RYA Boat Buye

Illustrations by Steve Lucas

©Graham Moody
First Published 2010
The Royal Yachting Association
RYA House, Ensign Way, Hamble
Southampton SO31 4YA
Tel: 0844 556 9555
Fax: 0844 556 9516
Email: publications@rya.org.uk
Web: www.rya.org.uk
ISBN: 978-1-905104765

A CIP record of this book is available from the British Library

Note: While all reasonable care has been taken in the preparation of this book, the publisher takes no responsibility for the use of the methods or products or contracts described in the book.

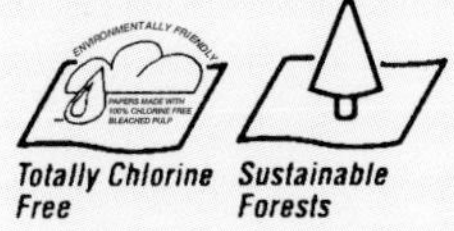

Cover Design: Jude Williams
Photographic Credits: Corby Yachts, Harken, Richard Langdon Skandia Team GBR, Melges, David Moody Collection, Motorcat, Orkney Boats, Richard Page, LDC Racing Sailboats, Sunseeker, David Harding Sailing Scenes, Avon Inflatables, Sea Otter Boats.
Typesetting: Creativebyte
Proofreading and Index: Alan Thatcher
Printed in China through World Print

During a lifelong involvement in shipping, business and yachting I have met a handful of people whose opinions and advice have been consistently sound and whom I have consequently learned to trust and respect; none more so than Graham Moody. With boat building and repair as his life's career and business he is extremely knowledgeable. In addition, however, what spare time he has is taken up by pleasure boating and racing. This experience, combined with an innate ability to solve boating problems and give sound advice on how to avoid them, makes him unique.
He helped me when a disastrous purchase of an old Whitbread boat forced a rebuild that, on a shoestring budget, presented a far greater challenge than the Whitbread Race itself. His assistance was invaluable. I try not to abuse our subsequent friendship by seeking his advice too often and this book will help me do that.

I have bought and sold at least twenty boats in my life, none quite as troublesome as the Whitbread boat but several were real headaches. Would that I had this book to hand – it could have saved a fortune in aspirin.

John Chittenden
Yachtsman of the Year 2001

Chapter | Page

If you are reading this RYA handbook, it is a fair guess you are considering buying a boat (maybe for the first time) or you are already the owner of a boat and contemplating a change. With the vast choice of boats on the market you are no doubt having a problem deciding which type and size of boat will best suit your needs and budget.

I cannot make the decision for you any more than I can stretch your budget. However, what I can do is provide you with information and advice which will allow you to make the most of your money and hopefully prevent you from purchasing a boat which will not meet your objectives. I will also try to prevent you from falling into too many unforeseen pitfalls, and incurring major expenses in the process.

Sailing yachts, motor boating, or simply messing about in a dinghy are wonderful pastimes which provide physical and mental exercise, the pride of ownership, numerous challenges and a complete break from the day-to-day stress of modern life. Boat ownership does, however, have its responsibilities; the safety of yourself, crew and vessel as well as other water users. So take care to select a boat you are confident in and a crew you can rely on.

This guide is divided into various sections and sub-sections. Even if you already think you know exactly the boat you want to buy, do read all major sections relating to that type of boat. Doing so will either confirm your original choice or help you find a more suitable alternative.

The RYA Boat Buyers' Handbook does not set out to teach you how to sail, navigate or operate your boat and its equipment. If you do not possess the skills required to operate your intended boat then I strongly advise you make every effort to acquire them before venturing afloat alone in your new acquisition, or to surround yourself with crew members with the necessary experience and skills.

CHAPTER 1

Objectives of Ownership

This is where it all starts. We all have reasons for wanting to own a boat; however, few of us make a list of them before we start looking. This often results in buying a boat which only meets one or two of our major objectives and does not fulfil many of our desires. Such a purchase quickly leads to dissatisfaction and the possible need for an early change of boat which takes time and, unless we are really lucky, costs more money. The worst-case scenario is that you get disenchanted with boating and decide to spend your well-earned leisure time and money on another activity.

OBJECTIVES OF OWNERSHIP

Some of your objectives may seem obvious; some are latent, and many require you to be really honest with yourself (and maybe with others). However, all should be considered. Below is a list of the most common objectives I have gained from years of experience helping people find their ideal boat. List your objectives in order of priority and make a dividing line between the top four or five, which are essential, and the others which, although desirable to you, are not vital.

Top Tip

- List your objectives of ownership and keep referring back to this list throughout the purchase process, to make sure what you are considering really suits your criteria.

To cruise
To cruise and occasionally race
To race and occasionally cruise
To race to win
To potter about in
To fish from
To relieve stress
As a style statement
To satisfy peer pressure
To promote family togetherness
As a retirement project
To live on full time
For exercise
As a DIY project
As a status symbol
A family decision
To find new friends
To keep existing friends
To use as a floating caravan
To charter
To fulfil a dream
To help in recuperation from an illness
To relax on
To long-distance cruise
As an investment
To coast = hop cruise
Pride of ownership
As a mobile property
Long-distance racing
To cruise inland waterways
For training prior to your ultimate boat
Other reasons

1.
2.
3.
4.
5.
6.
7.
8.
9.
10.
11.
12.
13.
14.
15.
16.
17.
18.
19.
20.

WEALTH WARNING!

Although I have seen boats sell for more than they originally cost, this is most unusual, so unless you are buying a boat at a knock-down price (confirmed as such by a reputable independent source), or you are an experienced boat trader, do not look on your boat as a short-term financial growth investment. However, by careful selection it is possible to avoid unnecessary dramatic losses in boat ownership (See chapter 10).

Having made and prioritised your list of objectives of ownership, continue to refer to this at each stage of your selection process to check how your favoured choice matches up. Look on it as a 'wish list' – if you have carefully thought out your objectives then boats you like should meet many of the requirements on your list. If this is not the case then reconsider, as it may need adjustment to reflect your revised desires. This could well occur as you reflect following reading chapters 2-7.

Remember: it is your boat and, although you are well advised to listen to wise heads, in the end the boat has to suit you, not your mates at the sailing club. **Your** boat must match **your** personal objectives if you and it are to have a long and happy relationship.

Top Tip

- It is your boat, your dream, your money and your choice, not that of your friends and advisors.

CHAPTER 2

Boat Type

Few people are heard in the yacht club boasting how slow or uncomfortable their boat is. To a cruising person space is very important, so some performance loss may be acceptable to achieve a better comfort level. As Uffa Fox said many years ago, "If she looks right she probably is right".

Many prospective owners will by now have already decided on the basic type of boat that they would like. However, some will still be undecided, to the extent that they have yet to choose between, for example, a round bilge, a chine motor boat, a racing yacht or a cruiser/racer sailing yacht. This chapter takes you through the salient features of each type of boat together with their advantages and limitations.

Top Tip

- Do not select a boat which is beyond your pocket, or you and your crew's size and anticipated skill capabilities, but do not undersell your ability to learn.

Motor Cruisers

For this guide they have been divided into four basic sub-types. Remember: when selecting a motor boat, pick one that looks like it was intended to be a motor boat, not a boat that looks like a sailing boat without masts.

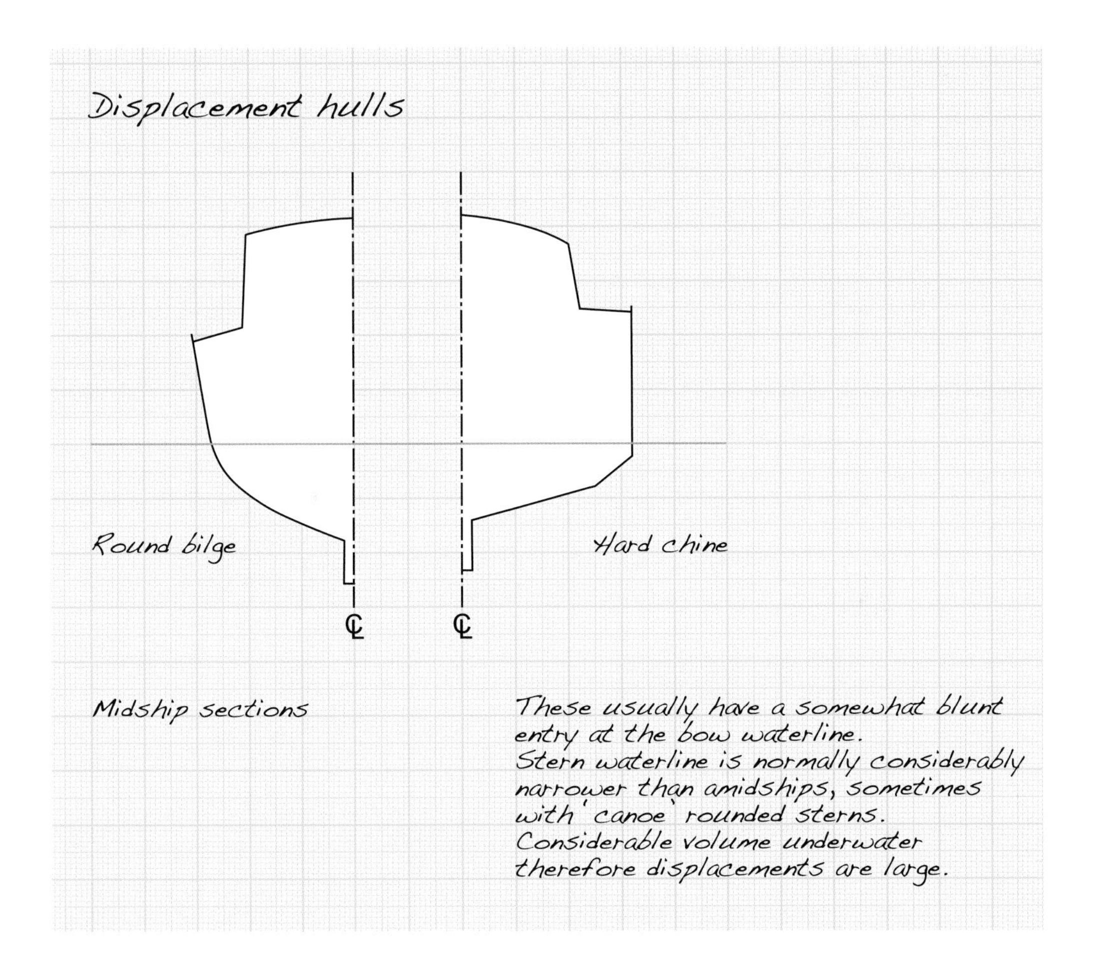

Displacement Type

These tend to be of a round bilge design – there are no sharp edges between topsides and bottom and they are usually relatively economically driven, with a low-powered engine. Most have a speed of 1.25 x square root of waterline length in feet. Therefore a typical 40-foot boat with a 36-foot waterline would have a maximum economic cruising speed of 7.5 knots, although she would probably go a little faster at the expense of disproportionate fuel consumption. Similarly, a 55-foot boat would have an economic cruising speed of 8.5 knots. Usually these boats have a round bilge hull form; however, many metal-hulled boats, despite being of chine or multi-chine hull form, fall into this category, as their weight makes it impractical to provide sufficient power to propel them at planing speeds, although this provides an economic method of construction.

- Space will usually be reasonable to good. However, as with most hull types, a fine forward waterline will give better economy.
- There is less wash and a better appearance at the expense of internal forward floor area.
- They make good long-distance cruisers and are a good choice for inland waterways, fishing boats and pottering boats.

Unfortunately, due to their lack of speed, they do not generate much dynamic stability when under way and, as a result, they do tend to roll. A good choice for the relaxed and economy conscious!

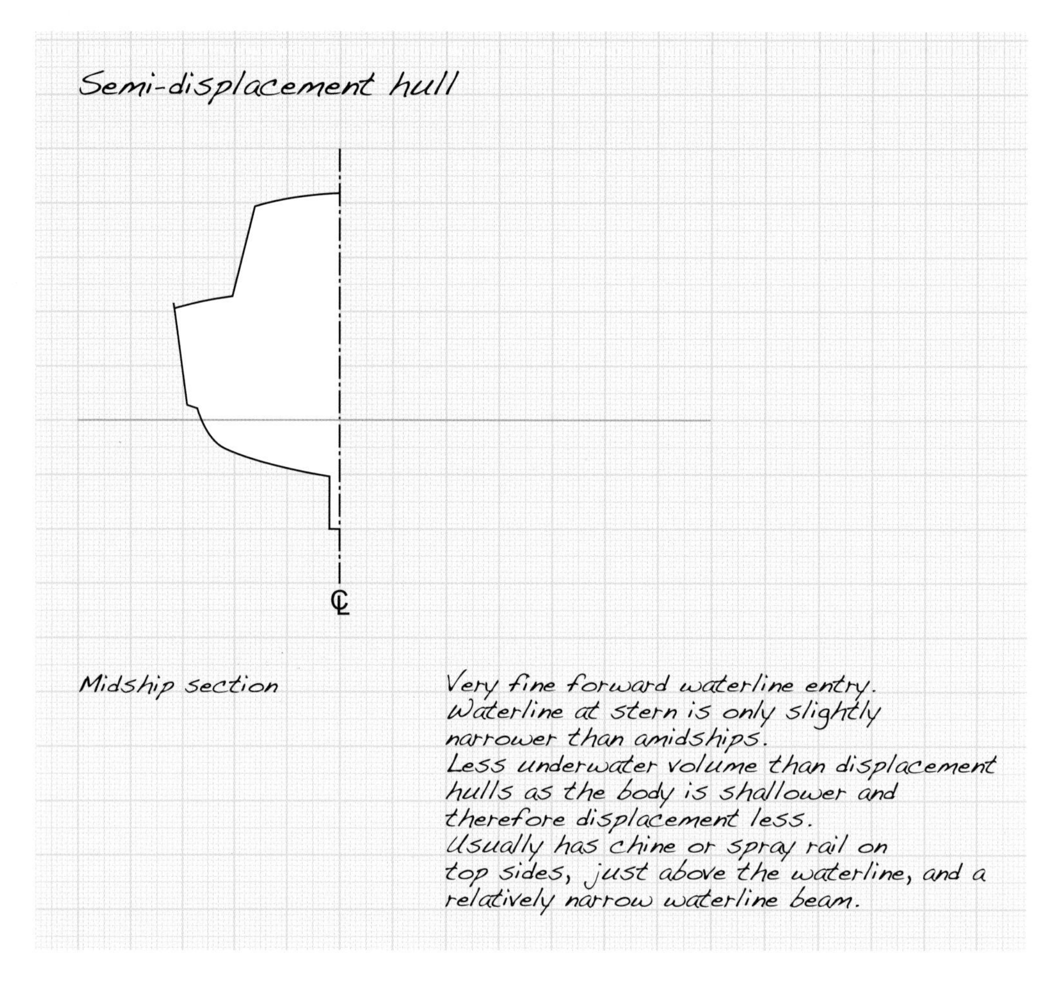

These are probably best identified as the type of hull form usually associated with pilot boats and fast lifeboats. They make excellent sea boats, particularly when powering into a head sea if a little wet. They also require skill and care in a strong quartering sea. Faster than displacement hulls, they achieve better dynamic stability at higher speeds. However, due to the high installed horsepower to achieve these speeds, they tend to be relatively uneconomic, particularly at lower speeds and at higher speeds in excess of 4 x square root of waterline length in feet.

- They tend to have a narrow beam/length ratio.
- Do not expect a large interior.
- Based on designs used by professionals.
- Usually coloured blue or white.
- Tend to hold their prices well.

Having an ageless quality, semi-displacement craft are seen as the choice of those who make an "I know a good boat" statement rather than a style statement, and are often the choice of retired racing sailboat owners.

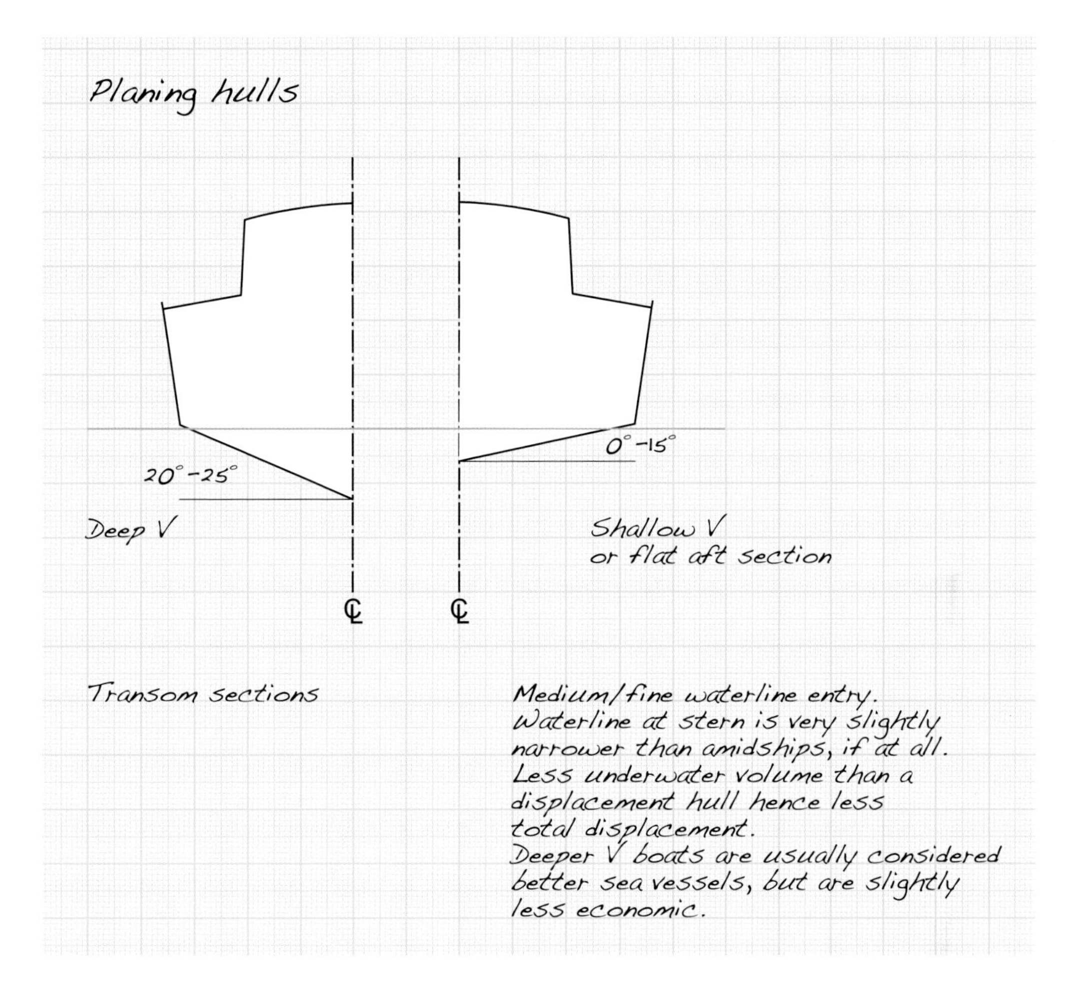

This section of cruising motor boats is by far the largest. However, it does tend to suffer from the vagaries of fashion and, although there are a few motor cruisers of ageless design, most tend to reflect current styling trends and as such are at risk of going out of vogue. This can be good news if you are a buyer, but bad if you are selling.

These boats have chine hulls, there being a sharp change of angle between topsides and bottom. They can be of flat bottom, medium or deep V hull form. This refers to the transverse sectional shape of the bottom near the transom. Usually, the deeper the V the better the sea-keeping qualities, but a deeper V can reduce performance and increase fuel consumption. The accepted norm is approximately 20-25 degrees between the transverse waterline and the hull bottom, a little less perhaps for cruising boats or a little more for sporty models. All deep V boats will require 2 to 4 spray rails to provide lift and dampen spray. These run fore and aft parallel to the centreline and should have quite sharp lower outer corners to be efficient.

Most modern planing hulls are of good design, providing reasonable to good sea-keeping qualities, assuming one is sensible with throttle settings. However, some from the 1980s or earlier were not so friendly. So, if considering an earlier boat, seek advice from an independent source. Avoid both under- and over-powered boats; the first will not maintain an economic cruising speed, the second will be costly to run and may well have been overstressed.

Top Tip

- While kit can be replaced and updated, a soft or weakened hull is difficult to stiffen up.

Accommodation will mostly be spacious. Some models concentrate on living space, some on large cockpits for entertaining or fishing and some simply on style.

Sometimes lacking in low-speed manoeuvrability or incapable of running within normal river speed limits (high-powered engines will object to continuous low-speed operation), this type of boat is not suited to inland waterway use. Relatively economic if operated just above her "hump speed", i.e. when she is planing cleanly (normally about 18-20 knots for a 40-foot boat), the most uneconomic speed is when she is half on plane (typically 13-17 knots for a 40-foot boat). However, do not expect these boats to be suitable for ocean crossing. Builders do not usually install large fuel tanks, because they would take up valuable accommodation space, are very expensive and would add considerable weight when full. This will sap away the top speed they can offer and require the installation of larger engines. For a typical 40-foot boat you will probably get a 200-300-mile cruising range.

- The speed range is normally 22-40 knots.
- Ideal for sunny climates and as day cruisers.
- Suitable for short-term living aboard only.
- Avoid those with less than a 25 knot maximum as they will probably have to run too close to maximum rpm to keep on plane. Heavy loads and/or a dirty bottom will make it difficult to get quickly onto plane.
- Avoid those with more than a 35 knot maximum, as they are likely to be very heavy fuel users.
- They do make a wealth statement.

If you want space, something a little stylish and you can accept the somewhat limited distance range, the need for a degree of weight control and some limitation on sea-keeping ability, a planing hull is a good choice, if only because there are so many to choose from. Eventual disposal should not be too difficult providing you are realistic on price.

If you are looking for a status statement then the sports cruiser versions of a planing-hulled boat could well be the choice for you. These tend to have larger cockpits, less accommodation, larger engines, be a little faster than the equivalent cruiser version, and have more 'racy' superstructure lines. Most tend to be well built to withstand the additional performance.

Sunseeker

Multi-hull Motor Cruisers

Only occasionally encountered in European waters but are widely found in Australia and New Zealand.

- Good accommodation space.
- Economic on fuel.
- If of a good design will have good speed.
- Tends to have an odd motion in any sea not directly in line with the direction of travel.
- If over 40 foot, will be expensive to berth and probably not road transportable.

These may be the cruising motor boats of the future, but not yet!

Motorcat

Sailing "Racing" Keel Boats

These fall into various categories. However, the splits between categories are not always easy to define. There are the "one design" classes, where normally the whole class sails with an equal rating, i.e. first to finish wins. There are the "level rating" classes, where boats of different designs are sailed using the same rating, various factors such as sail size being adjusted up or down to achieve the stipulated level rating figure and, again, the first to finish wins. There are handicap races, where boats of different ratings and designs sail the same course, their elapsed times to complete the course being multiplied by their handicap to give a corrected elapsed time. This is compared to other entrants' corrected times to give the race result. Class boats and level rating boats can usually also compete in handicap racing.

There are various rating systems, IRC being the currently most widely used. Others are IRM, IMS and, for dinghies, Portsmouth yard stick.

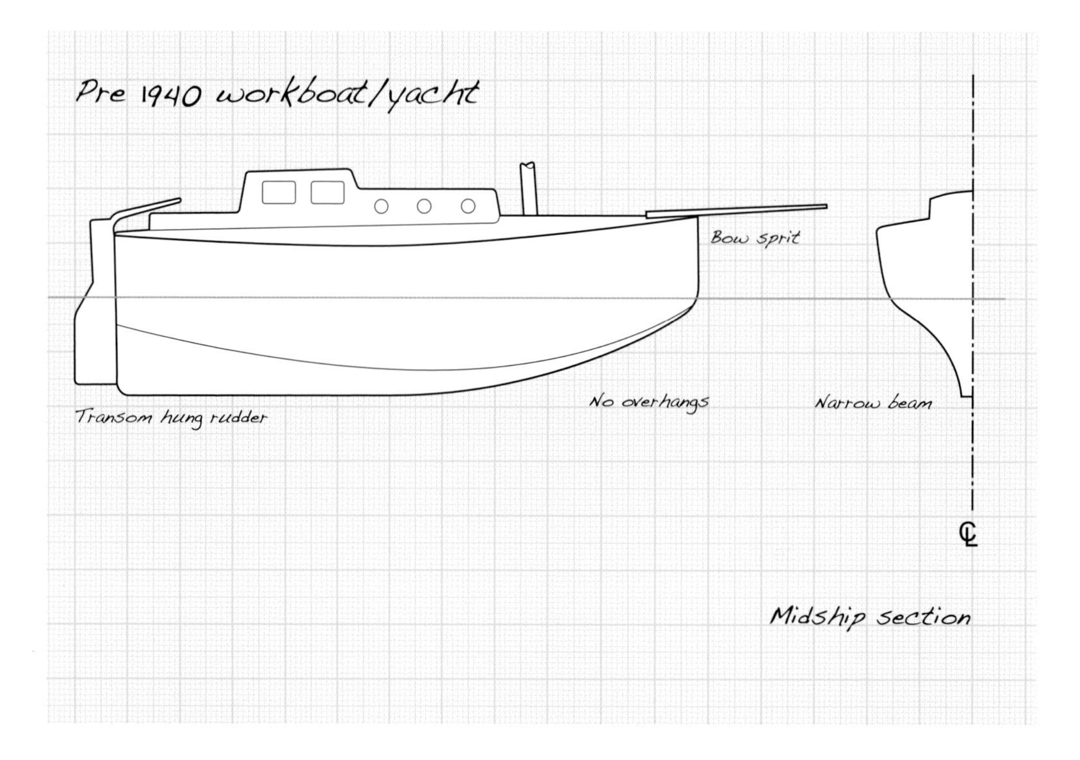

Accommodation on a racing keel boat tends to be sparse. Boats built before the mid-1980s may be a little better served in this respect, as the older rating rule then in vogue was inclined to handicap light displacement severely. Recent designs below 30 feet (9.5m) do tend to have very little in respect of overnight crew comforts. This reflects their use mainly as day sailers with the occasional overnight passage race. However, in 2008, the IRL raised the penalty on stripped-out interiors.

When selecting a racing keel boat, other than your budget, the major factors to consider will be the level of design complexity to suit you and also your crew's capabilities. Some boats are very difficult to sail well.

"One designs" tend to be a little more restrained. To win you will still have to be good, but they are usually a bit more forgiving than a "one off", "state of the designer's art" boat, which will shine in the experts' hands, but can frighten the less skilled, who will probably not be able to keep her consistently in the groove.

Size is important, as to race well you will need a consistent, reliable crew. If you know you can only count on, for example, 5, do not select a boat requiring 8. Also, is her draught practical for the area in which you expect to sail, and can you be sure of a mooring or shore storage space for her? Is there a suitable fleet to compete against and a good race calendar?

Avoid unpopular designs – there is probably a good reason why they are unpopular. Unless you feel you can assemble the necessary design and sailing skills to make this phoenix rise from the ashes of her past failure, even then proceed only if you can buy her at a price which reflects her shortcomings.

In addition to national one-design classes, there are now several builders' level rating classes which could be worth consideration. One advantage of choosing a boat with sister ships is that she is more likely to have an established owners' club. Additionally, in-use development will have tended to have taken place and been incorporated into later builds. Any one-off boat may not yet be fully sorted. Some may be seen as a challenge, others as a risk.

One area which is currently providing good racing at reasonable cost for the capable is in the classic, mini, quarter, half and one-ton classes. However, you have to be either knowledgeable or know someone who is to avoid buying a failed design or a boat in need of a major rebuild.

Always check both the history and condition of a racing keel boat. If she has failed to perform before (except one-design boats) why do you think you can now do better? All racing boats which have been seriously sailed have been heavily stressed. Some designs can withstand this but some are built a little closer to the limit and may need attention. Be wary of any rigging on a hard-campaigned boat over 3 years old. Always get a second-hand racing boat surveyed, preferably by a surveyor with experience of her type.

If considering buying a new racing keel boat, you can commission a new design. This is great as each new design is an opportunity to take development further, but you have to accept the risk that she will not be a winner and the resale value could be questionable. Alternatively, you could opt for an established design. Look at her sister ships to see what kit works and how to best tune her for results.

To consistently do well any boat will need good, consistent crew, good sails and the kit to be correct, well sorted and understood. A well-sailed but average boat will occasionally do well, a poorly sailed good boat may be lucky on the very odd occasion, but there is only one way to ensure regular good results – have a good boat, know her well and sail her better than the opposition.

Cruiser Racers

Much of what is written above applies equally to cruiser racers. In fact, some would argue many "one-design" classes are cruiser racers. My opinion is that a cruiser racer is a boat, which in addition to being raced is comfortable and docile enough to live on for at least a week, sailing from "A" to "B" without the need of a full racing crew, leisurely and without hassle.

Corby Yachts

So what does a race boat need to be a useful cruiser racer?

- The ability to be sailed by probably fewer than half of her racing crew number (without drama), accepting that some may be less experienced.
- Reasonable sleeping, cooking, food storage and washing facilities, a degree of privacy and comfortable seating.
- She will also probably need larger fuel and water capacities and bigger batteries than a pure racing boat. This all results in extra weight which will have to be removed before racing, or the inevitable light wind penalty accepted.

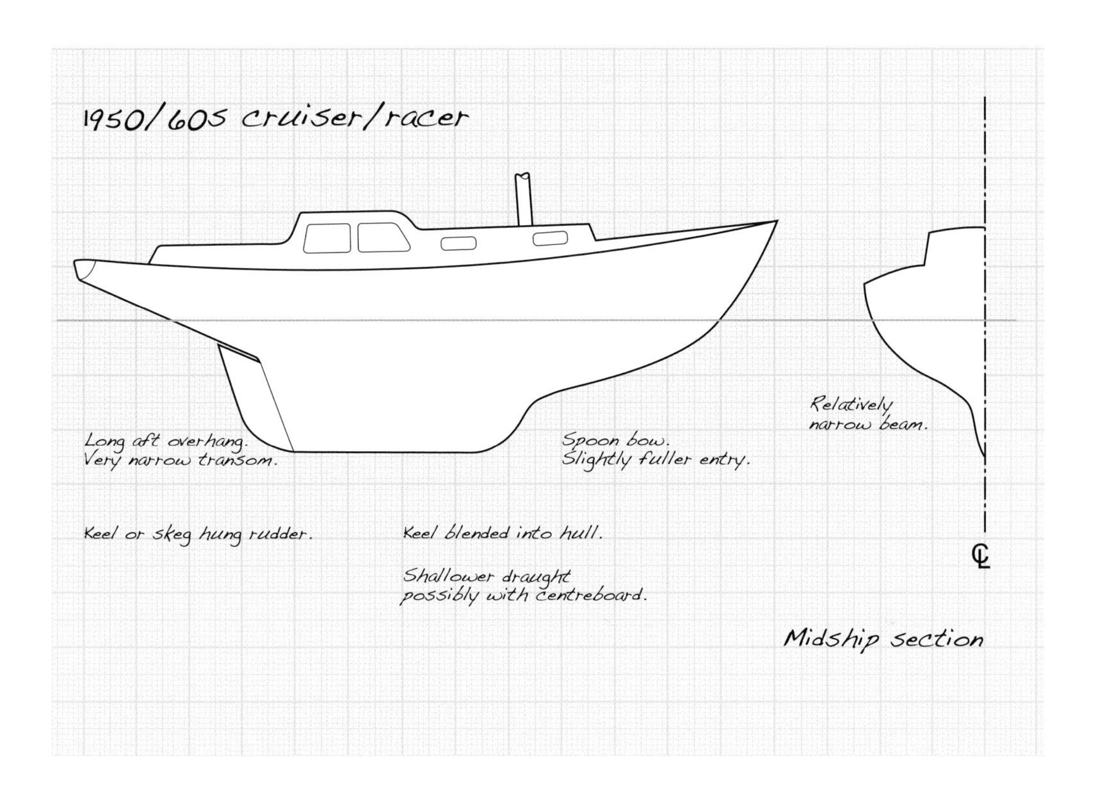
1950/60s cruiser/racer
Long aft overhang.
Very narrow transom.
Spoon bow.
Slightly fuller entry.
Relatively narrow beam.
Keel or skeg hung rudder.
Keel blended into hull.
Shallower draught possibly with centreboard.
CL
Midship section

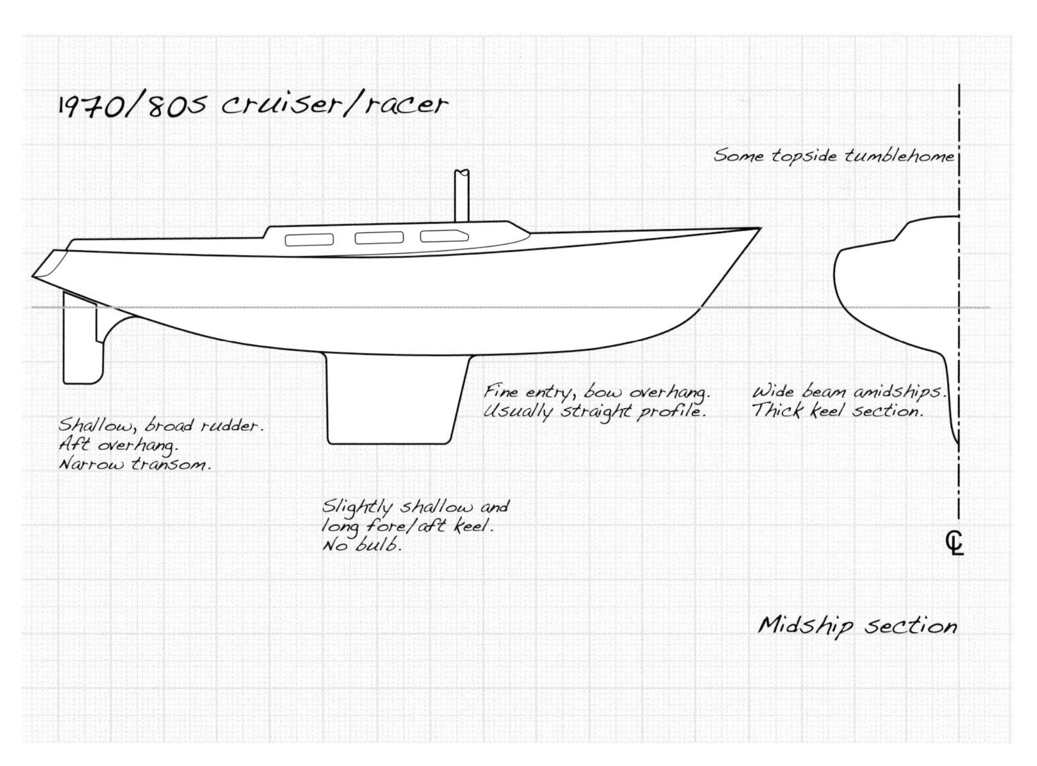
1970/80s cruiser/racer
Some topside tumblehome
Fine entry, bow overhang.
Usually straight profile.
Wide beam amidships.
Thick keel section.
Shallow, broad rudder.
Aft overhang.
Narrow transom.
Slightly shallow and long fore/aft keel.
No bulb.
CL
Midship section

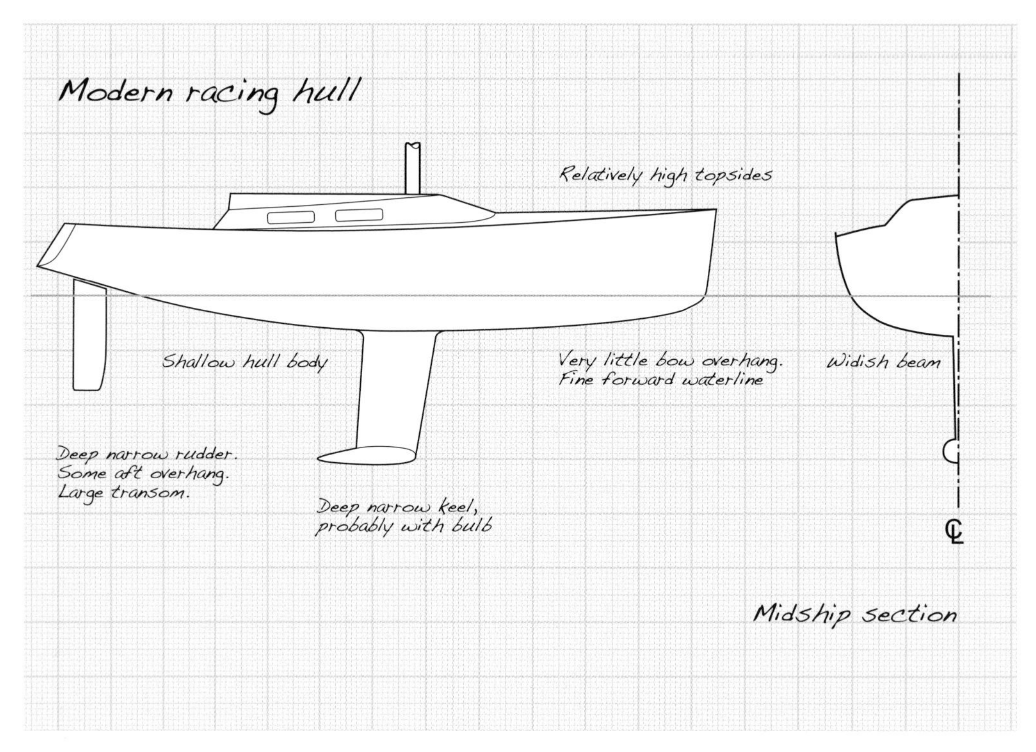

In the past, old retired racing boats used to be converted to cruiser racers. Modern "all-on" racing boats are more critical to sail and do not usually adapt so easily to becoming successful cruiser racers. However, do not despair, as recent design and materials development means it is possible to build a cruiser racer capable of good club-level performance, not overburdened with excess weight, and fitted for comfortable cruising.

You will have to decide where your priorities exist when selecting sails etc, as you will almost certainly want a series of separate headsails to race competitively, but the simplicity of a roller reefing jib for cruising. There will be many other compromises and choices. The best answer is, if you can afford it, to have both cruising and racing kit, swapping as your usage dictates, as you will find the kit for one use often unsuited for the other.

Harken

Cruising Keel Boats and Motor-sailers

Just as with the cruiser racer you will have to decide on your own priority level between performance and comfort. Comfort for living aboard equates to more weight, which detracts from sailing performance, as greater weight means more underwater volume, usually a fatter boat, and more power being required to achieve the same speed. This is not a problem when motoring, as you can simply fit a larger engine and propeller, but a big engine means more fuel and a big propeller more drag when sailing.

When sailing you will probably want an easily handled rather than optimum-performance sail plan. You will neither accept the additional sail area required to offset the extra weight nor the deep draught to give the best windward results. So all cruising yachts are a compromise, but getting the compromise right is as difficult a challenge for the designer and builder as producing a top-performing racing boat. Cruising implies longer trips at sea, so the creature-comforts requirement increases.

David Moody Collection

Cruising boats can range from the sailing boat with a small motor for docking and emergencies only to the full bodied motor-sailer with sails only suitable for off-wind performance or steadying roll, but a big powerful engine(s) for all but ideal sailing conditions. Neither is right or wrong; they are both suited to the individual needs of particular owners.

Cruising boats will tend to have fewer sleeping berths than racing boats of similar size. A 45-foot racing boat would typically have 10-12 berths, one for each member of her rated racing crew, whereas a cruising boat of similar length would have 6-8 berths, which would be split up into separate cabins, providing more privacy and personal space. A 45-foot cruising boat would probably have two toilet compartments, whereas a racing boat of this dimension would possibly settle for one in order to save weight. In a cruising boat you could expect a shower, a refrigerator, possibly heating and air conditioning, a deep freeze, bow thruster etc, all of which will require larger batteries and fuel tanks, plus possibly a generator to make her independent of shore power.

Racing boats are almost always sloop rigged, as this has proved to be the sail plan which gives the best all-round sailing efficiency on the full combination of points of sail. When cruising, you can choose to avoid sailing hard to windward, either electing to wait for more favourable weather or by putting on the motor. As windward performance is now of a lower priority, consideration may be given to different rig layouts. This also allows the sail plan to be divided into smaller, more easily handled sections. For this reason many cruising boats and motor-sailers may have cutter, ketch, yawl or schooner rigs.

In these days of full electronic navigational aids, almost all boats have reasonable chart table areas, but the electronic fit will vary between a racer and a cruiser. Both will have the basics, but whereas the racer will probably have a program including sailing polar graphs, tides and wind information, the cruiser will probably include radar and more specialised communication systems.

David Moody Collection

Cruising boats do not need to be as weight-conscious as racing boats. This tends to result in the quality cruising boat being strong, with a long life expectancy, resulting in high resale values. The first production cruising boats I built around 1970 sold for approximately £12,000 – today they fetch approximately £25,000 on the second-hand market. Unfortunately, not all cruising boats on the current market are built with excess strength to help shrug off the occasional light grounding or berthing error. They do, however, meet the current legislation. So if buying new, be a little wary of cruising boats of low price and weight. These lighter boats will probably survive their early life without serious problem, their economic build only manifesting itself after a few years. This is why they may look to be bargains on the second-hand market (but not to their first owner). If considering an economy cruiser, even if only a year or two old, it is important to have a proper survey before purchase.

There are now some good, strong multi-hull sailing cruisers available. These are probably better suited to the Mediterranean and Caribbean than northern European waters; they give good deck and accommodation space but suffer from an odd motion at sea and berthing will be both costly and scarce.

Before selecting a cruising boat or motor-sailer, list the principal requirements as set out below, then check these off against the models you are considering:

- Number of crew.
- Minimum range under power.
- Maximum size you are confident with, or which will fit the harbours you intend to visit.
- Any draught restrictions, water or air.
- Maximum anticipated time at sea without shore support – this will determine storage required and some kit (i.e. generator).
- The intended cruising area – this will indicate possible weather and temperature you will experience and influence your mix of deck/interior space.
- Your choice – mainly sail, 50-50, or mainly motor.

Class Sailing Dinghies

The first choice you have to make is whether you are going to sail alone or with a crew.

The advantages of single-handed sailing are:

- You can sail at your own convenience, not being restricted by crew availability.
- Single-handed boats are usually light and simple to rig, so preparation time and pack-up times are reduced.
- They are small and light, making them easier to transport and store.
- You and you alone are responsible for winning or losing.
- Single-handed boats are relatively economical to own and to campaign seriously.

Richard Langdon Skandia GBR

The disadvantages of single-handed boat ownership are:

- They are not particularly social whilst afloat.
- You have no one to blame but yourself for poor results.
- They lack the "soul mate" association of a crewed boat.
- As they are usually simply rigged, there are fewer things to tinker with.
- You will have no crew to call on to assist with maintenance and to share costs.

The advantages of a crewed boat are:

- They are normally a little larger and more complex than a single-handed boat.
- You and your crew can bond and develop your skills together.
- You can share boat set-up, breakdown maintenance, and possibly costs with your crew.
- The range of crewed boats available tends to be wider so it should be easier to select a model which exactly suits your aspirations, abilities and weight.

The disadvantages of a crewed boat are:

- You will have to find a crew of the right skill level, or one willing to learn or teach, who can be relied on to turn up and help with preparation, maintenance etc, and occasionally buy a drink at the club.
- You will have to be compatible with your crew – this does not mean you will not have disagreements but that you will respect each other.
- As all dinghies are designed for a particular total crew weight you will have to choose boat or crew to suit. If not, you run the risk of ending up having to be either a light- or heavy-wind specialist boat.
- You can only sail when all crew members are available, or you will have to cultivate spare crew capacity, but chopping and changing crew is not a good route to efficiency.
- Due to their size and complexity a crewed dinghy is likely to be more expensive to buy, store and run than a single-hander.
- Crewed boats are heavier, with a more complex rig set-up. Launching, recovery, de-rigging and maintenance will require the assistance of your crew, and transporting your dinghy may require a larger car.

Having decided if you are going to have a single-handed or crewed dinghy, you should next choose which class best suits your needs. If you are an experienced sailor you are probably already a member of your local club; if not, I suggest you look to join now. As there are so many different classes of sailing dinghy, all clubs tend to specialise in races for a small selection of particular classes, so that their members can experience good level-rating racing. However, clubs also run handicap races to allow other classes to race.

David Harding_Sailing Scenes.com

See which classes are raced where you intend to sail, then check which of these suit your skill level and weight. Picking a locally established class should not only provide you with better, more competitive racing, but will also give access to accumulated tuning and sailing knowledge related to that class in the conditions prevailing locally and will eventually provide a wider market for disposal when you move to your next boat.

If you are on a tight budget you could consider buying a less popular class. Check, however, that it is suitable for use in your location (it may be unpopular for a good reason, i.e. it is a lake boat and your club is on the coast). Classes which used to be in favour but have gone out of vogue locally are often a decent economic prospect as there will probably be a good supply of cheap spares available. If you are learning a class new to you, but one which has been established for some time, consider a good second-hand boat as an interim project on which to build your skills and carry out your tuning experiments.

If you are tempted to buy a particular boat because she has had an excellent past racing record, unless her last owner is selling her to move to another class ask yourself why she is for sale. Has she been overstressed? As with all local boats, discreetly ask around the club, ask only those you can trust and those who are experienced in the class in question.

Before making your final selection of a class, ask yourself the following questions:

- Can I (we) afford to buy and campaign this boat at the level which would make me (us) happy?
- Have I (we) selected a boat suitable for my (our) weight and skill/fitness level?
- Is there a strong local fleet?
- Where will she be stored and how will she be transported?
- What are my (our) exit options if for any reason I (we) do not get on with her?
- Is there a class association I should join?

Speedboats, PWCs, RIBs and Fast Inflatables

This group of boats is probably best summed up as planing craft below approximately 26 feet (8m) which are primarily used for getting from "A" to "B" but have no meaningful accommodation. These craft have many uses, some being bought for more than one use. They can be operated as fun boats, ski boats, fishing boats, yacht tenders, work boats, dive boats, picnic boats, commuter boats and safety boats, among other things. Each type has its use; some are more suited to certain operations than others, but equally all have their limitations. Some can be raced, some are only suited for short, fun trips in sheltered waters and some are capable of serious heavy-duty use. It is vitally important that you pick a type suited to your intended needs.

Richard Page

Speedboats

These are the basic concept from which all of the following types evolved. The concept is a smallish boat which can achieve high (20+ knots) speeds, being relatively light but strongly built and powered by a low weight/high power output motor. Although those built in the past tended to be somewhat fragile and not always endowed with good sea-keeping qualities, modern materials and improved designs mean most current models can be expected to have a reasonable life expectancy if restricted to their intended use and maintained well.

I would advise against considering buying any of the remaining plywood speedboats unless they are in exceptionally good condition and your intended use is on flat water lakes. Mostly built before 1980, due to the materials used they are now beyond their expected working life.

There are a few aluminium alloy speedboats around and, in fact, some are still being built. The older ones tend to be collectors' items, while the newer ones are usually aimed at the commercial market. Strong but a little less swish than GRP equivalents, they also are noisy in choppy seas.

GRP is by far the most commonly used construction material for speedboats. If buying a second-hand boat, particularly an older one, check the hull carefully for cracking and grounding problems. If you find any, consult an expert in GRP to confirm how serious the damage is.

Speedboats come in many shapes and styles, from open work boat/tender to very fast, plush models. They have various hull forms, from flat-bottomed aft for use on flat waters only to deep V aft for coastal use. They can also occasionally be found in multi-hull form, which is good for space and low wash. One particular hull form worthy of mention is the cathedral/dory type. These are good for space and load-carrying, better than a flat bottom in a chop but probably not as comfortable as a deep V in a head sea. One oddity of this type is they often have double skin hulls with foam in the void, making them, their makers claim, "unsinkable". One drawback of this construction is they tend to be more expensive to repair than a conventional hull. If safety is of paramount importance to you, this may be an acceptable price to pay, but check second-hand examples carefully.

Advantages of speedboats:

- They make a good (if well selected), inexpensive fun, picnic or fishing boat and a style statement for the younger, less well financed.
- There is a wide market so you should be able to find what suits you relatively easily and in due course dispose of her equally easily.

Disadvantages of speedboats:

- Overtaken by their offspring in popularity and practicality in many roles as listed below.
- They are less fun than PWCs, less forgiving and generally less seaworthy than RIBs, and heavier than rubber dinghies.
- Ensure that the installed engine falls within manufacturer's recommendations. There should be a notice fixed to the boat giving this information.

Personal Watercraft (PWCs)
This recent addition to the range of small, fast craft is primarily designed as a fun boat. Usually small, at 10 feet (3m) or less, each can carry 1, 2 or 3 persons as designed, is manufactured from GRP or plastic, has a factory installed petrol engine coupled to a waterjet drive, and can be of either sit-on or stand-on design.

Advantages of PWCs:

- Great for their limited intended purpose, the waterjet gives a degree of safety to swimmers and is less susceptible to grounding damage than a conventional propeller.

Disadvantages of PWCs:

- Only suitable as a fun or surf rescue boat, the small size makes for a tiring ride in a sea way.
- They have received much bad press due to a buy and use mentality, as opposed to a buy, learn and then use regime.

Rigid Inflatable Boats (RIBs)

Developed in the 1960s and 1970s these boats combine the sea-keeping qualities of a deep V hull with the safety and bump resistance of a rubber boat. There are now many different styles and makes available and performance is usually good – RIBs are raced and have completed trans-ocean passages. They are built in varying lengths from approximately 10 feet (3m) upwards, are powered by outboards, inboard/outboards and waterjets, and are petrol or diesel fuelled.

Advantages of RIBs:

- Safe, bump resistant, good sea-keeping in almost all models.
- Variety of layouts and styles available to suit all tastes and uses.
- Ready market, good popular RIBs hold prices well.
- Relatively easily repaired.

Disadvantages of RIBs:

- Some early models did not have good collars (the blow-up bit) or good hull/collar attachment.
- Some have been intensively used as work boats.
- Some have limited space/seating.
- Popular, so a bargain may be hard to find, but a fair deal should be readily attainable.

Fast Inflatables

These are boats which have no permanent rigid hull structure so they can be deflated for transport and storage. They are usually between 8 feet (2.5m) and 17 feet (5m) long, outboard powered, with either a plywood or inflatable floor. Although used as lifeboats for inshore waters, they are not recommended for extended use in anything other than calm conditions.

Advantages of fast inflatables:

- Light, easily transported and stored, they make good yacht tenders, as they are a fender and cause little bump damage.
- Relatively inexpensive as new.
- Safety – they are, after all, halfway to a life raft.

Disadvantages of fast inflatables:

- Short life (approximately 10-15 years) means high depreciation.
- Usually wet and to a degree flexible – not good except in reasonable conditions if you want a comfortable ride.
- Can be vulnerable to impact damage with sharp objects.
- Not advisable for use in rough conditions, except by fully trained persons.

With both RIBs and fast inflatables, attention to inflation pressure is important; under-inflation results in a soft flexible boat, reduces performance, shortens life and detracts from ride quality and safety. Over-inflation also shortens life, and risks bursting. Check that you keep within manufacturer's recommendations. Remember that an inflated tube will vary considerably in pressure with temperature; a tube which feels soft on a cold morning will feel considerably harder in the midday sun, but turn soft again in the cool of the evening. So do not pump up too hard when temperatures are low and high temperatures are expected on the same day.

Avon Inflatables

Fishing and Pottering Boats

This group comprises boats designed for this purpose, and those designed as motor cruisers, sailing cruisers and speedboats adapted to this new role. Most are motor boats but some have secondary sails provided.

The typical boat size for pottering is 33 feet (10m) or less, but may be a little larger for fishing purposes, particularly in areas subject to rough weather, or for extended use. This is, I would like to point out, pleasure and not commercial fishing.

If you are looking to buy a converted boat, or convert one yourself, care should be taken to ensure that any existing or intended modifications from the original design do not compromise the structural strength, alter her stability, or make void any operating approval she has previously been granted. Typical problems are:

- A cut-down transom to accommodate an outboard motor, resulting in the risk of flooding.
- Built-up superstructures, reducing the righting moment.
- Poorly installed, untested gas systems and generally worn-out equipment.

If you intend to fish from the boat you will need a cockpit large enough to allow space for the number of fishermen, typically 5-6 feet of cockpit edge per person. A good, safe anchoring arrangement and sea-keeping capabilities suited to your intended fishing area are also important.

Pottering and fishing are often perceived as the poor relations of motor and sailboat cruising; they may be in respect of financial investment, but in enthusiasm and pleasure derived from these activities they are far from being so. There is, however, a note of caution which must be sounded. Many, but not all, pottering and fishing boat owners do undertake their sport on limited financial resources and unfortunately this sometimes leads to a degree of neglect of maintenance and safety issues.

When considering buying a used boat in this group, take special care to ensure all equipment, as well as the boat, has been properly serviced, or allow for this in your post-purchase budget. A pottering or fishing boat is at just as much risk of being caught out in bad weather or experiencing unexpected dramas as any other boat and should be properly maintained and fully equipped to best mitigate any situations which may arise.

Orkney Boats

CHAPTER 3

Budget

Only you know what you can afford, or, if purchasing as a syndicate, what the group is prepared to spend. One cannot put a percentage of income or personal wealth as a guide, as we all put our boating activities at a different level of priority. I have known some owners who deem their boating to be of greater personal importance to them than spouse, children and home and, whereas I may envy this dedication, I do believe in some degree of moderation.

One can always use loans or marine mortgages to finance boating and in many instances, when a steady income is assured, this is a sensible method of purchase. Do not forget that any loan or mortgage may be called in if you default, so ensure you reduce risk to the minimum.

I cannot set the quantum of your available budget, but I can give you the information which will allow you to budget more accurately for pre-purchase costs, purchase costs and early ownership costs.

Top Tip

- Do not kid yourself as to total cost. Add purchase, upgrade, servicing, storage and insurance costs together, and then add a contingency sum for unforeseen expenses.

Up-front costs: These are the costs occasionally overlooked as they tend to come out of your pocket rather than directly from your bank account. They include purchase of books and magazines to help in your selection; travel to inspect boats, clubs and sailing areas; hotel costs; training costs; club and/or class association and RYA membership fees; specialised personal clothing and safety equipment costs, and survey costs (when budgeting allow for two or three surveys, as if the first boat fails the survey, or you are outbid, you will need to repeat the exercise).

Actual purchase costs: The accepted price of the boat; any initial financing charges; any costs in respect of putting the boat into an operating condition, such as launching, stepping masts, equipment, operational checks and instruction; vital repairs to bring to a safe working condition so that you may move your new boat to her normal berth; road or skippered transporting costs if applicable; personal travel and living costs incurred in achieving this situation; necessary operating licences or permissions needed to operate the boat, and finders' or other possible professional fees, including your accountant's and solicitor's costs if you have involved them. All of the preceding costs are, I contend, part of the purchase price, as without them you do not have an operating boat.

Essential upgrades: These are the costs you deem essential to incur for you to feel that the boat is ready to undertake the activities you intend. The boat as you bought her will probably not fully meet your needs and these are the costs involved in updating the boat from a basically seaworthy vessel as set out in "Actual purchase costs" to one which more fully meets your requirements. The difference is that you may accept deferring these expenses for a short time, whereas the "actual purchase cost" is essential early expenditure prior to use. This group would include replacement sails, anti-fouling (but not anode replacement), new non-vital electronics, new comfort systems, air conditioning, layout revisions, and cosmetic improvements, but not the purchase of new essential safety equipment, which must be part of the "actual purchase costs".

Running costs: These are the repetitive costs which are necessary to operate your boat. They include: boat insurance; crew insurance; registration fees; light fees if applicable; regular survey costs (including gas systems); safety equipment and life rafts, life jackets etc; regular finance costs; regular, plus visiting, berthing fees; radio licence fees; harbour dues; anti-fouling; anode replacement; engine servicing; sail and rig repairs; essential gear replacement (as old equipment reaches the end of its reliable life); valeting; fuel; gas; water; race entry fees; class and club annual membership costs; charts; almanacs and other necessary publications; winter storage; consumable chandlers' items; clothing replacements, and probably many others, possibly individual to you and your boating style.

You should also make a contingency allowance for the almost inevitable occurrences not covered by insurance, or specifically budgeted for. My proposal is this: the emergency sum should be approximately 25% of your annual budgeted costs and, for smaller boats, a minimum of £200. This money can be left on deposit in an instant access account. I make this proposal as I believe it will go a long way to relieve stress and panic if the unforeseen occurs.

With different types of boat, different parts of the budget will assume greater significance. A speedboat's budget will show fuel as a major item whereas a racing sailing boat will probably major on sail expenses. List your anticipated budget costs using the above as a guide for your initial type and size of boat, then compare this with your intended spend. From this first comparison you should be able to take a considered view whether your initial desires fall within your financial limitations, or if you should consider amending your target boat. If this is so, repeat the exercise.

When you get to the shortlist stage it may be prudent to revise your budget for each of your target acquisitions. Budgeting is not an exact science; it is an educated guide as opposed to an uneducated guess. It is only a tool to help and should be considered an aid to avoiding making the wrong decision, rather than a method of making the right one. The right boat is that which meets your objectives of ownership, not necessarily the one which exactly matches your financial situation. A boat which is too rich for you is unlikely to make you a happy boater.

If you are considering some form of joint ownership, you are entering an area which has led to the break of many a long friendship. This is totally unnecessary, providing those involved are prepared to be honest in respect of their own financial situation and all parties clearly write down and sign their obligations and rights. In larger boats this is probably best executed by a solicitor (potentially another cost to budget for), but one which may in smaller, less expensive boats, be served by a simple exchange of letters, provided they cover all reasonably foreseeable areas of concern. Shared ownership agreements should include the split of initial investment between the parties; distribution of maintenance and running costs; obligations to assist in manual and organisational work; a commitment to emergency unforeseen costs; rights and limits of usage; individual responsibilities, and not least an exit programme to allow any party to move on. This is not a complete list as circumstances will be individual; it is simply a guide.

If you are intending to buy either a new or used boat, most budget considerations will still apply. With a new boat, although your equipment-purchase costs may be higher, depending on standard specification, your early replacement costs should be lower, and warranty cover may mitigate most breakdown expenses for at least the first year of ownership.

Some costs which may occur, but could well be overlooked are:

Rigging replacement: Most insurers insist on standing rigging being replaced at between 10 and 15-year intervals. However, serious racers who regularly load their rigs to near their limits and long-distance cruisers who cram several years' normal mileage into a short period should consider earlier replacement (see page 51 for further details). From this it can be seen that knowledge of a used boat's history is important.

Equipment: Engines and electronics may look and be in good condition at the time of purchase, but could be long out of production and an early breakdown may result in requiring a replacement, due to spares not being available. Some older outdrive legs are particularly difficult to obtain spares for.

Gas systems: These should be regularly tested by a qualified engineer and issued with a system safety certificate – ensure your intended boat, new or used, has one.

Osmosis: The bane of pre-1980s GRP boats and occasionally seen in later models (see page 33 for further details). If found, you or the vendor will have to meet the cost of remedial treatment.

Sails: These wear out so you should consider their survey by a sailmaker, plus possible repair, valeting or replacement costs.

Anti-fouling: Over the years this is applied coat on coat and, after 5 to 7 re-coats, the old, dead original coats begin to flake off. After 10 years most boats require the complete removal of all old coatings.

Batteries: These typically have a life of 3-7 years, depending on original type and quality.

Finally, when setting your budget level, be honest with yourself. Are you one of the few "who live to sail", or are you someone for whom boating is enjoyable but just one of several areas of spending?

CHAPTER 4

Build materials

Boats are built from a range of materials. Some are in vogue, some older materials and technologies are fading from use and there are of course new materials which may or may not pass the test of time.

Top Tip

- Every construction material and method has its advantages and drawbacks. Check which are best suited to your intended use.

Glass Reinforced Plastic (GRP)

This is by far the most common current construction material because it lends itself to series production. Although expensive to tool-up for, it is far less so than the cost of making the tooling necessary to produce a series of boats from pressed metal panels, as used in car production. Cars are built by the thousands, boats by the tens or hundreds, and therefore spreading the cost of tooling and development has to be over a smaller number.

GRP comes in many forms. Strictly speaking the name implies glass reinforcement but in fact many different reinforcements are used to bind the resin, including in addition to various qualities of glass matt and rovings, aramids such as Kevlar®, carbon, expanded porous foams etc. In fact, GRP is probably better termed Fibre Reinforced Plastic (FRP). The resins also vary; where originally only polyester resin was widely used, now vinylester and epoxy have widespread use. Polyester underwent a major improvement in the early 1980s from orthophthalic to isophthalic formulation in an effort to reduce the risk of osmosis, which is simply the passage of a liquid through a membrane and which in boats resulted in blistering and, in severe cases, luckily few, weakening of the structure.

Like all other forms of construction there are excellent, good and poor examples of GRP boats. Quality is unfortunately not uniformly good. If you are not sure ask “the informed” if your intended boat’s builder has a good reputation which has stood the test of time. There are, for all types of construction, minimum structural requirements to which a builder must work to allow him to put his product on the European market.

These rules endeavour to ensure that all boats are safe at the time of going into service. Racing and cruising boats are built to the same rules. Racing boats are used to their limits and therefore any defects in structure soon become obvious, so builders/designers take care to avoid weaknesses without increasing weight. If defects become evident, early modifications to rectify faults are instituted. As cruising boats tend to lead less stressful early lives this accelerated in-service testing is less evident.

Safety and long-life conscious, quality builders ensure their cruising boat structures receive care equal to their racing boat structures and make allowances for long life and minor impacts with dock and seabed. Some builders realise they can build a light structure economically for cruising boats, which, whilst meeting the letter of the rule, fails to have the reserves of strength which I believe are necessary to provide a cruiser with a long, trouble-free life expectancy.

There are three ways to identify these boats, which do not, I believe, make good long-ownership prospects as cruising boats:

- Weight. This is not so critical in a cruising boat, so if the boat you are considering is lighter than others of similar size ask why. Is this the result of good high-tech design or building down to a price?
- Price. New or second hand – if the price is less than competitors, are you buying less?
- Reputation. Ask "the informed" but take the salesman's spiel with "a pinch of salt".

Top Tip

- A lighter weight can mean greater speed for a sailing racing boat, but a shorter life for a cruising yacht.

Fortunately this situation seems less prevalent in the motor boat field, possibly because most motor boats would soon show up weaknesses due to the loads imposed by water impact at the speeds at which they travel. For motor boats, the poor hull form of some mainly earlier designs is normally of greater concern than structural shortcomings.

GRP has facilitated the volume production of boats more than any other material. All GRP boats have an outer skin called the gelcoat which is usually self-coloured and, as such, avoids the need for secondary painting of the above-water external surfaces for many years. Although coloured gelcoats look good when new, white gelcoats are the better bet for long-term good looks as they do not suffer the effects of ultra-violet rays and oxidisation to the extent that blues and reds do.

If buying a second-hand GRP boat I recommend a survey by a suitably qualified surveyor. However, some quickly observable defects to look for are:

- Impact damage having broken through the gelcoat.
- Distortion of the hull shape caused by a lack of adequate hull stiffening, poor blocking off when ashore or in transit.
- Hull cracks as a result of impact with seabed, dock or other boats.
- Star cracks (they look like spiders' webs) are usually the external evidence of an internal impact.
- Blistering which may or may not be osmosis. If when burst they are found to contain small quantities of a vinegar-smelling liquid, osmosis is a strong possibility.

All GRP boats benefit from a few weeks ashore to dry out each year. If buying second hand, ask if this has been the case with this boat and, for new or old, adopt this practice to protect the value of your investment.

Wood

The traditional material still has much to offer, but only for the true enthusiast who has the time and money to maintain this material properly, or soon an investment will become a liability. There are many old wooden boats maintained in good condition, some well over 100 years old. However, during their life most have had major sections of their structures replaced. Proper wooden boat maintenance requires extensive skills that take a long time to acquire and are thus expensive to buy. However, a well-maintained wooden boat probably produces the greatest "pride of ownership".

There are several methods of wooden boat construction. Plywood was used extensively up to the 1980s but has now faded in popularity with professional builders, although some amateur examples are still produced. Unless plywood boats are very well maintained their life tends to be limited to approximately 15-20 years and any boat older than 15 years should be very carefully inspected. The main areas of concern are the edges of individual ply panels, the solid wooden battens at panel intersections, the stress points where fittings are attached and the plywood itself, as less expensive plywood quite often shows signs of delamination. Should this occur, the only reliable solution is to replace the panel, which is not always an economic option due to the relatively low value of boats of this construction.

The traditional construction methods with wood were carvel, where solid wooden planks were bent along the length of the boat and fastened to an interior framework, resulting in a smooth finish, and its main alternative, clinker construction. Here the planks were again run fore and aft and attached to an internal framework but, instead of being fitted side-by-side, the planks were overlapped and fastened to each other through the overlap, rather like overlapping fence panels. This method produced a stepped appearance to the planking and tended to be used on smaller boats. Both methods require knowledge and skill to maintain and repair and are probably beyond the average DIY enthusiast's skill level to work on.

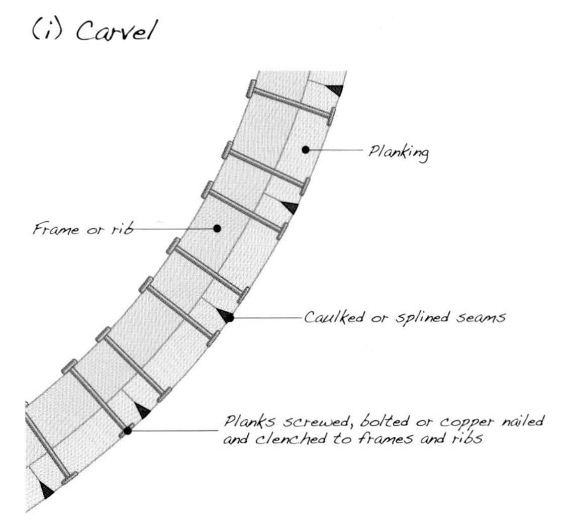

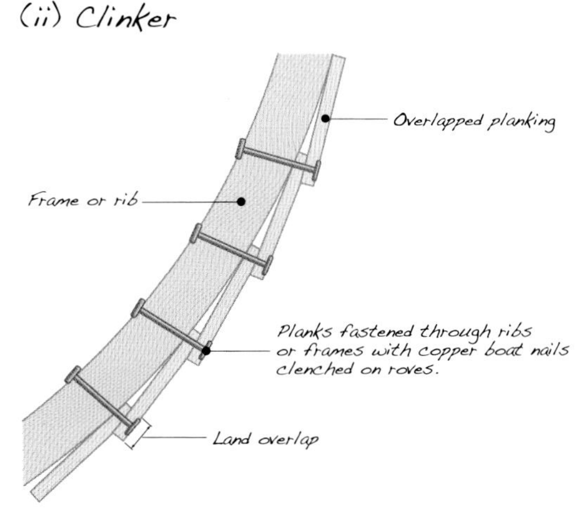

(iii) Moulded (hot or cold)

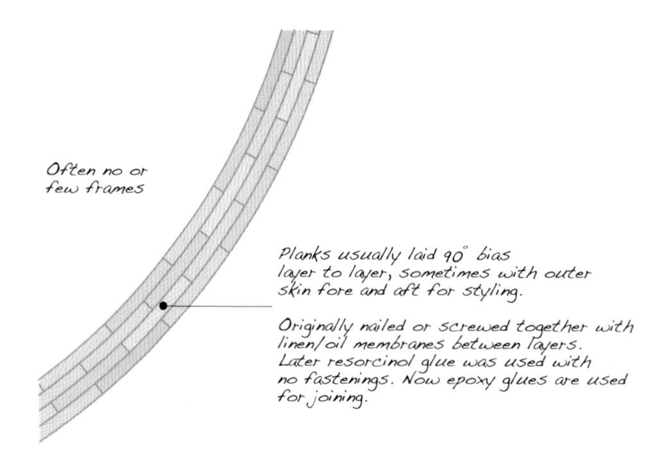

Since the 1940s glues have existed which have allowed boats to be built using veneers glued on top of each other. With the advent of synthetic glues such as epoxy, not only did adhesion and glue life improve but the impregnation of the glue into the wood acted as a very good preservative. There are two main types of this form of wooden boat construction – hot moulded and cold moulded. Hot moulded is not used very much now; it produced a very strong boat but required an expensive autoclave oven similar to that now used for formula one racing car chassis built in carbon fibre. The first of these were in fact manufactured by boat builders.

Cold moulding, where no oven is required, is still occasionally used in one-off development boats. Cold-moulded boats of considerable size have been built – I was personally responsible for one of 168 feet (51m), which may be the largest ever. However, before the popularity of GRP was established, this was a major building method and good examples can still be found but should be inspected by a specialist prior to purchase.

Plastic Boats

Many smaller dinghies are now produced from plastic using injection spin, vacuum or hot deforming methods. These methods are only suited to volume construction due to the tooling costs involved and have not yet featured in larger boats. They tend to be self-coloured and not suited to later painting. If of good quality they are strong and have a reasonable life expectancy, provided they are protected from the effects of ultra-violet rays when not being used.

Metal Boats

These are mainly of steel or aluminium alloy construction. Steel is favoured for canal boats because it can withstand the inevitable impacts they experience. It is economic to produce and repair, particularly if single curvature shell plating is used, which is common on inland waterways boats where the weight penalty usually associated with steel is acceptable. Long-distance cruising boats, both motor and sail, can also tolerate this weight penalty as their size mitigates the effect. They also benefit from the security of the strength of steel. However, as they usually have flowing lines, single curvature construction is not an option so they are plated with double curvature panels, which requires higher skill levels and more expensive machinery. For these reasons and the cost of fairing and painting to good yacht standards, steel cruising yachts do not feature at the budget end of the market. Most steel cruising motor boats are found in the over 47 feet (14m) size range. Just as wood rots, steel rusts and, in older or less well-constructed versions, life is a constant battle against this problem. Dissimilar metals also lead to corrosion, so a good survey and great care with modifications is strongly advised.

Aluminium Alloy Boats

These are still produced in small numbers, mainly from one-off designs which cannot accept the weight penalty of steel due to performance requirements. There is however, a limited number of production boats built, tending to be for a specialist market. Aluminium alloy is more difficult to work than steel for, whilst it is more easily bent, it stretches on bending more than steel does and is more difficult to weld structurally. These high skill levels lead to expensive building costs. Alloy does not corrode from salt water as badly as steel does, provided the right material grade is used. However, it suffers even more than steel from corrosive effects resulting from adjacent non-compatible materials. Well designed cathodic protection is vital on all metal boats to protect against corrosion, which can be a major cost to correct.

Concrete Boats

Now a rare build material, they found a degree of favour between 1960 and 1980, but are inclined to be heavy and of compromised performance. Many were of amateur construction with suspect standards. There are no doubt a few reasonable ones still around, but my advice is that unless you are an expert or have access to one, steer clear.

Rubber Boats

The name is probably not correct but everyone knows inflatable boats by this name. They make ideal tenders as they can be deflated and packed away. They also take the form of a large fender so they tend to cause little damage to topsides; most have multiple inflation chambers so they have a high level of safety in this respect. As they are very light, however, their sea-keeping qualities, if lightly loaded in strong seas or winds, are suspect.

Life rafts have water ballast tanks to combat this but they are not built to be propelled. Price dictates both quality and life expectancy. There are some inflatables 25 years old but these are the exceptions, most have a much shorter life, often the result of neglect. They are relatively easily repaired but repairs will be evident. To prolong its life, wash regularly, dry and talcum powder dust over before extended storage and keep covered to avoid ultra-violet rays.

CHAPTER 5

Size

In purchasing, boat size can be of great importance. The exception is if you have decided on a particular one-design racing sailing boat, when the class rules will dictate the dimensions. One thing is certain, the operating costs of a boat are proportional to her size. The larger the boat, the more expensive she will be to maintain and berth.

If you have a minimum number of family or friends with whom you intend to share your boating then this will dictate the minimum size of boat required to accommodate them. The longer the trips you intend to undertake, the more space you should allocate to each person. Where 8 people may be content to be together on a 35-foot (10m) boat for a short trip, it is unlikely they will all be happy to sleep aboard; 6 or 7 may, however, be prepared to live aboard for a night or two, but for a week's cruise, 4 or 5 is probably the maximum. You must be careful not to exceed either the recommended maximum crew number or safety equipment provision.

Top Tip

- Size is important! Too small will be cramped, but too large could exceed your budget limitations, berth size and crew availability.

Maximum size may also be dictated by various factors: available berth dimensions; the need to be road transportable; water depth; air clearance under a bridge; local restrictions; your qualifications; yours and/or your crew's level of competence; local maintenance facilities, and, last but not least, your budget.

It may be prudent to buy a slightly smaller, less expensive boat to ensure confidence that you can keep her in good seaworthy condition and actually be able to afford to use her occasionally.

Sunseeker

If, however, one of your objectives for buying a boat is as a status symbol, then the bigger the better if you can afford the associated costs. Do not be tempted to buy big but cheap as this will not give the image you require. It is most important that you select the right size to meet your objectives, and that you can afford and operate your boat. Be careful when selecting a boat by size as not all builders use the same method of arriving at their advertised length. Some motor boats include overhangs such as pulpits at the bow and built-in bathing platforms at the stern. This can considerably increase the advertised length, although not inaccurately because the boat does extend to these extremities, and this is the length you will probably be charged in a marina. This can be misleading as these extensions do not add to the accommodation space. Some builders give a length more related to the true bow to transom dimension. In this case, a boat of a smaller advertised size could in fact be of greater usable length.

Some sailing boats have long overhangs which, although making the boat more elegant, add nothing to the accommodation. It is probably better to compare sailing boats based on similar waterline lengths than on overall length, as this is more likely to result in boats with similar internal space.

Top Tip

- Waterline length gives a better indication than overall length as to internal space.

CHAPTER 6

New or used?

Do not rule out either option too early in your selection process, as you may well find a nearly new boat with most of the optional equipment you require at a good saving on new price. Similarly, if believing you can only afford second hand, you may miss a really good deal on, for example, an ex-demonstrator by simply not looking at the new market.

If you are buying a racing sailing dinghy to race at national or international level, you are best advised to consider buying new, as used boats could well have been stressed, distorted, become overweight due to soaking up water, or become soft. You must be honest with yourself as to your potential. Most of us believe we are capable of being the next Olympic champion despite being overweight, short sighted and not particularly skilled.

Sunseeker

Advantages of buying new:

- You will get at least a year's warranty, which should limit some of your early running costs and risks.
- Your boat should have all current specification equipment.
- You can select exactly the optional equipment you require, not being tied to a previous owner's choice.
- You will have the pride of ownership of a shiny new product.
- You may be able to get the sales company to make a deal including some options at no or reduced cost.

- If you do not have a berth (they are difficult to obtain in some popular locations), you may be able to make provision of a berth, if not its cost, as part of your agreement to proceed with purchase.
- There will be no unanswered questions as to past history.
- Your boat should meet all current legislation.
- The title should be less open to question.
- You can expect several years of reasonably low costs as you start out with zero running hours on all gear.

Disadvantages of buying new:

- The initial cost is usually higher than an equivalent used product.
- Early yearly depreciation levels are normally much higher than those from, say, 3 years old and onwards.
- Sometimes there is limited equipment in standard specification.
- Some sorting and tuning will need carrying out. All boats tend to have a few snags and whereas your dealer will no doubt sort them, they can be frustrating.
- The inevitable disappointment as the newness wears off.
- The fear of scratching a new toy.
- If your choice is an untried new model, there is the risk of her proving a failure and with this unpopularity comes a compromised resale value.

Advantages of buying second hand:

- Discounted purchase price compared to new.
- Probably a much enhanced equipment specification.
- All teething problems should by now be sorted.
- You can afford a larger boat for the same monetary outlay.
- The possibility of buying a berth with the boat.
- Lower future depreciation to look forward to.

Disadvantages of buying second hand:

- Little prospect of a guarantee unless the seller is a marine company owning the boat, possibly as a part exchange from a new boat sale. Most used boats are sold either via brokerage agents acting for the owner but not owning the boat themselves, or privately. In both instances it is unusual for a guarantee to be provided.
- The possibility of unforeseen faults, not noticed or not evident at survey.
- The need to invest money in a survey to provide peace of mind that no major problems exist.
- The specification could include out-of-date equipment, possibly with no spares available.
- Some gear which has been kept well maintained, such as standing rigging and batteries, could still be approaching its replacement date.
- The need to accept the previous owner's choice of gear, colours etc, or to pay for replacements to meet your needs.
- The difficulty of knowing if you are getting a reasonable deal is always a problem in a small market place, an almost impossible one when contemplating purchasing a used "one-off" boat, or an unpopular class, when few comparisons can be made.
- Having to accept often uncertain past maintenance level history.

Only in a few cases is it possible to be categoric on the decision to buy new or used.
In addition to the very competitive dinghy racer mentioned above, new is probably going to be the preferred choice of the owner who knows exactly what he/she requires but cannot find it on the second-hand market, the person who cannot contemplate buying anything previously owned by another, and by someone who has selected a new design for which no second-hand market currently exists.

Top Tip

- Do not rule out buying either new or used until you have researched the market.

The only people I can think of who have no choice but to buy used are those who want a genuine classic boat, someone who has decided on a boat which best meets his/her objectives of ownership only to discover that the model in question is no longer in production, the person with larger requirements than his/her budget will allow on the new market, and the owner who gets his/her enjoyment from renovating older boats.

CHAPTER 7

Equipment

The two most important considerations are firstly that your equipment choices match your objectives of ownership, and secondly your budget limitations. If intending to cruise inland waterways, radar is unlikely to be high on your shopping list, but good fendering will be. If racing, your spending should be directed at items which will aid boat speed, and if cruising, towards creature comforts. However, one area no-one should ignore is safety equipment.

I propose that, after reading this section, you list your equipment requirements in three categories – essential items, worthwhile items, and nice to have but not necessary items. When you have shortlisted boats you can compare each to these equipment lists to gauge the level of additional spend over the actual specification offered within the sale price. You may also consider putting a budget price against each item on your list. This will allow you to calculate quickly the total cost of each boat on your shortlist against your requirements. Do not forget to include installation costs where appropriate, as well as equipment purchase costs.

Top Tip

- Remember that installation and commissioning costs should be added to purchase price.

Many items can be purchased at different quality and sophistication levels, often greatly altering cost. You should decide from your priority list where you need the best available equipment and where working efficiency is all that is required. If you are racing a sailboat, high-tech sails will probably be a must, despite their relatively high cost compared with the standard Dacron® sails which will be adequate, if not better, for a cruising boat. Just as on a cruising motor boat, although a standard GPS will suffice, it is unlikely that many will now accept less than a coloured chart plotter. I give below a short guide to various areas of equipment. Some may not apply to your particular choice of boat; however, I hope you will find it helpful when compiling requirement lists.

Top Tip

- Check service and spares availability on existing installed equipment.

Safety Equipment

Important for all boats, safety equipment must reflect the number of crew and the boat's intended use.

Remember that safety equipment, although vital, will not guarantee a problem will never occur. It is there to reduce the secondary consequences of problems, should they unfortunately arise.
Good maintenance, preparation and seamanship are what help to avoid accidents. As the unforeseen will happen, especially at sea, the proper safety equipment is essential for you, your crew and to assist others.

Top Tip

- The unforeseen does happen at sea, so check your safety kit is adequate for your intended use and crew size.

Some sailing venues, classes and all race rules impose minimum safety equipment-carrying limits. These are not maximum allowances and if you believe it is prudent to carry more, do so. Similarly, even if you are not bound by these restrictions, remember they have been formulated by experienced boaters and I recommend the cruising owner refers to the racing safety equipment list for his/her size of boat as an informed guide.

I list below some of the items you may require, depending on your boat size and type, as a checklist.

Navigation lights.
Emergency navigation lights.
Spare bulbs and batteries for navigation lights.
Torches.
Signal lamp.
High-powered torch.
Spare batteries and bulbs for torches.
Fire extinguishers.
Fire blanket.
Buckets with lanyards attached.
Bailer.
Bilge pumps – hand type with handles attached or stowed adjacent.
Bilge pumps – powered types, electric or engine driven.
Fire pumps (mandatory on larger yachts) and hoses.
Portable VHF radio.
Rockets and flares and/or Very pistol.
Anchor and rope or chain plus on larger boats an anchor winch.
Spare anchor and line.
Tow rope suited to boat size.
Life ring(s) and lights and holders.
Quoit or throwing line.
Dan buoy.
Harnesses and lines (with two clips).
Ships' emergency breakdown spares and tools.
Radar reflector.
Storm sails.
Emergency water and food.
Emergency steering.
Emergency knife.
Mirror (for sun signalling).
EPIRBs.
DSC/VHF Horn.
Emergency aerial for VHF.
Emergency clothing and/or thermal blankets.

- Life jackets – at least one for each member of crew, including children's sizes, if children included in crew. If boating other than only by day, or if not only on inland waterways, complete with reflective strips, whistles and lights plus possibly for deep-sea use dye markers, mini flares and personal EPIRBs. All must comply with current legislation. Give serious consideration to gas and automatic inflation.
- Life raft(s), including appropriate internally stowed kit and proper stowage brackets. Total raft spaces to be at the very least, the maximum number of crew.

This is not an exhaustive list!

Engines

Almost all boats other than sailing dinghies, canoes, pulling dinghies and a few classic boats are now equipped with some form of engine or are capable of having an outboard mounted on them. Any engine is only of use if it is properly selected for the boat to which it is fitted and is reliable in operation.

A non-functioning engine is at best expensive ballast, or at worst a safety risk.
Engines come in many types, either classified by fuel used or installation method, and also by power produced. The fuel types are diesel, petrol, two stroke mix petrol, liquid petroleum gas (LPG), electric, occasionally steam or paraffin and, more recently, hydrogen fuel cell, but for this guide, as they are so rarely encountered, we will ignore the last three.

Installation types

Inboard: This is where a shaft with the propeller directly attached passes through the underwater hull skin and the motor is mounted inside the hull.

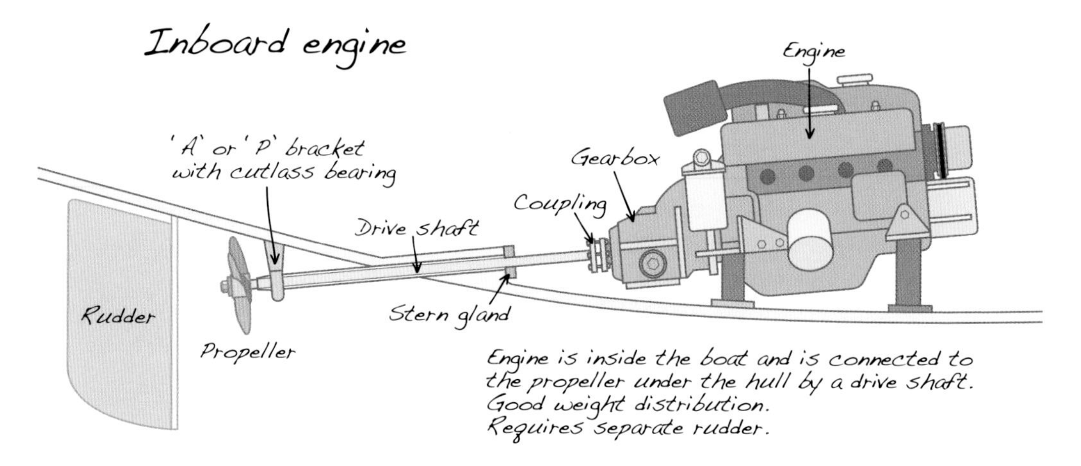

Outboard: This is where the motor and its drive system are one unit, hung on the boat's transom.

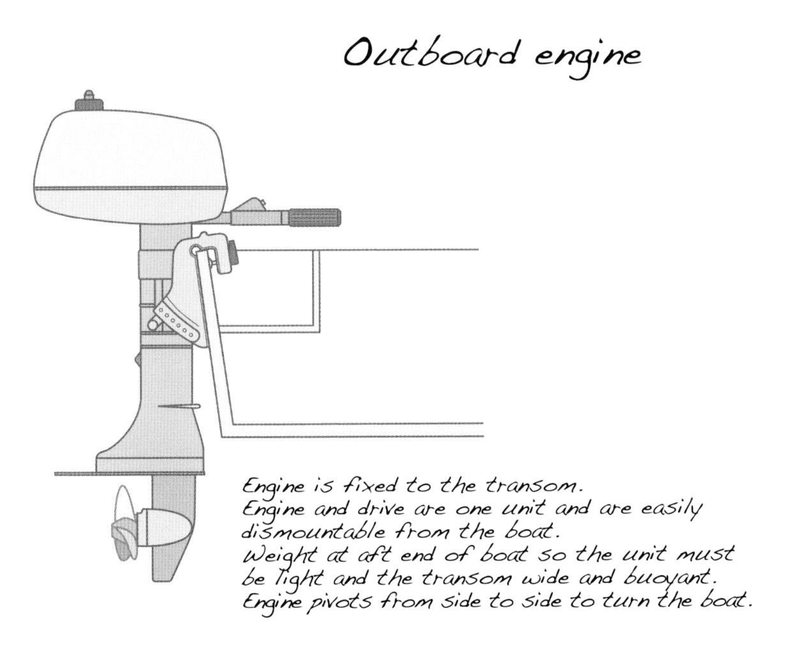

Inboard/outboard: These have the engine mounted inside the boat with the drive passing through the transom to a propeller system mounted behind the transom.

Inboard/outboard engine

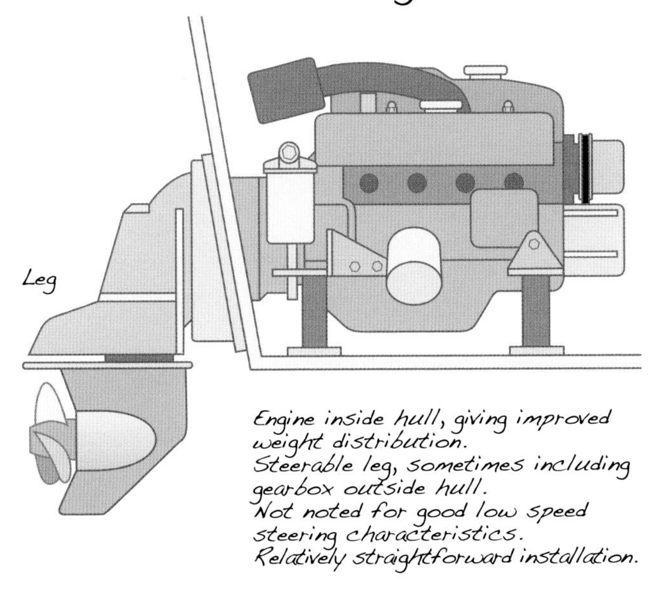

Water jet drive: Here the motor drives an impeller pump which draws water in through the boat's bottom and ejects it through the transom.

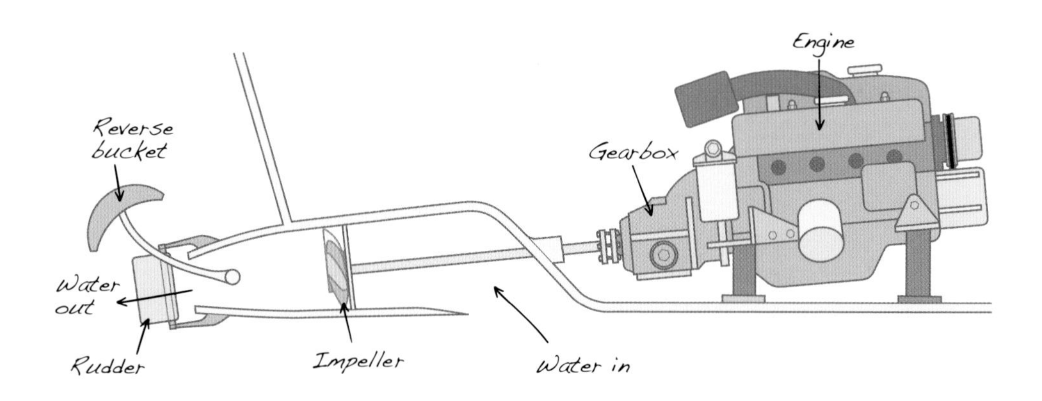

Leg drive: Here the motor is situated inside the hull and connected through the bottom hull skin to a drive leg similar to the lower end of an outboard.

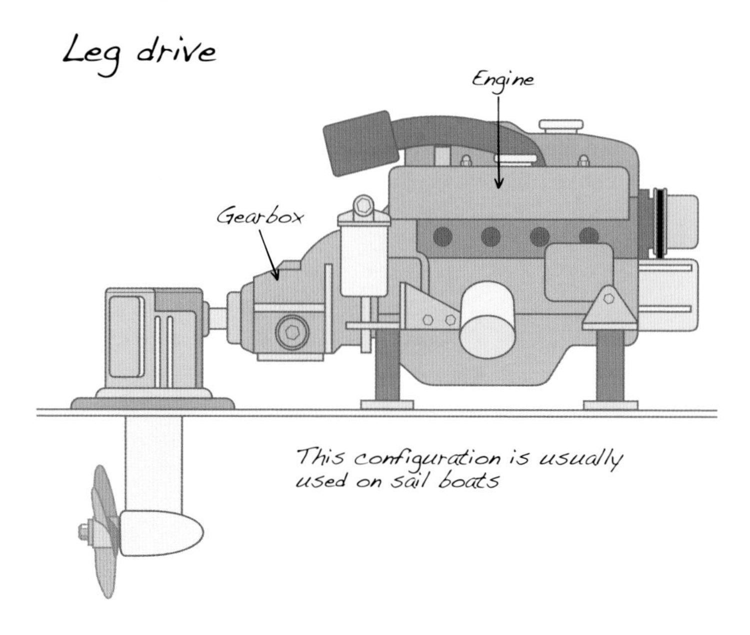

For this guide I will ignore paddle wheels, pure jets and mechanical rowing devices.

When comparing engines, they are given power ratings expressed in horsepower. However, there are several different standards and some powers are measured at flywheel and some at gearbox output, so check you are comparing like for like. Gearbox horsepower will always be less than flywheel horsepower due to friction losses in the gearbox.

Most engine manufacturers now quote a common standard of rated horsepower but some older engines may have their power shown in standards producing a higher figure than current ratings. If you are powering a fast boat, horsepower is important, but if your boat is of a heavier displacement type then torque rating is equally important. A two stroke outboard will tend to have high horsepower but low torque, making it suitable for a speedboat, however a slow revving diesel with high torque and relatively low horsepower will be better suited to a displacement cruiser.

Personal watercraft are weight conscious. They are usually powered by lightweight petrol two or four stroke motors connected to jet drives. These need careful maintenance, regular flushing with fresh water to avoid corrosion, and are not noted for long trouble-free lives.

Speedboats and RIBs use a variety of engine types and drive systems – engines are listed in ascending order of perceived quality and life: two stroke outboards, four stroke outboards, petrol inboard/outboards or jet drives, diesel inboard/outboards or jet drives.

Rubber boats tend only to use outboards. Small to medium (24-40 feet, 7-11m) motor cruisers of the planing type may use petrol, diesel or LPG-fuelled outboards, inboard/outboards, water jets or inboards. The engines will be of good power to weight ratio. Larger motor cruisers are normally powered by four, or occasionally two stroke diesels, usually on shaft drive but in rare instances, water jet, leg or surface propeller drive systems. Semi-displacement boats will normally have diesel shaft drive systems but may have inboard/outboard or water jet drive systems. Small sailing boats may use outboards but this is unusual in boats over 30 feet (9m). These usually have a small diesel or petrol engine on a shaft or leg drive. Larger sailing boats are usually diesel powered with shaft or leg drive, but it is not common to see leg drive on boats over 48 feet (14.5m). Inland waterways boats use most types of engine but these are of lower power due to their limited speed requirements. As charging connections are available and low noise and pollution is valued, electric drive systems are starting to become popular, mainly on smaller craft. Fishing and pottering boats can incorporate various motor and drive options, as some are fast and some are slow boats.

It would be unusual in the UK to find a boat over 39 feet (12m), with anything other than diesel power. This is for several reasons – diesel is a lower fire risk, consumption is less than petrol so range is improved, modern diesels have quite good power to weight ratios, diesels are seen as more reliable partially because they do not have water-sensitive ignition systems. The only drawbacks are that diesel engines are a little noisier and a little more expensive.

Due to European pollution legislation two stroke outboards are becoming less common. They also err towards being less fuel efficient than their four stroke relatives.

A good engine will only function well if it is correctly sized to suit a boat – too small and performance will suffer, too big and it will be too heavy, restrict space and could cause safety and handling problems. Most smaller boats fitted with outboard motors, which can easily be substituted, have a manufacturer's plaque giving the maximum permitted power. This is carefully calculated for safety; check it is not exceeded, as if it is your insurers may not be keen to meet any claim. If it is necessary to replace an installed engine it is best to match as near as possible the original power and weight specification.

All boats' performance is reduced by two commonly ignored factors. The first is fouling of the hull bottom, which can easily cause up to a 25% loss in efficiency if not worse, so good anti-fouling and regular scrubbing in some high-growth areas and in hot weather are important to maintain speed and range. The second is propeller condition. This is important as a mismatched or damaged propeller can drastically reduce efficiency. If in doubt, consult a specialist.

Range

Range is an important consideration. The day excursion boater is unlikely to require more than a six-hour duration as it is probable he will be able to top up daily. Range applies to speedboats, inland waterways boats, small sailing cruisers, and pottering and inshore fishing boats. In fact, owners of most PWCs and speedboats may well have a much shorter duration. Fast motor cruisers will typically have a range of between 200-300 miles at cruising speed (usually 21-24 knots). This may not seem a great distance but fuel is heavy and storage takes up space.

Weather, bottom fouling and excessive speed can all reduce manufacturers' advertised range, and the wise skipper always allows a safety margin. There are some fast motor cruisers with better range capabilities and if your planned trips are likely to require longer between stops, select a boat with enhanced range.

The high-performance engines fitted to fast boats are designed to run at about 75% of their maximum engine speed for long periods, not at low revolutions, where they are not being efficiently fuelled. Use at low revolutions for long periods can result in engine damage, particularly on new engines, where the cylinder bores may glaze. Slower motor cruisers and sailing boats with auxiliary engines have a much longer duration in time at sea, as they consume much less fuel per hour.

Smaller boats (36 feet/11m or less) will normally have a range of between 100-250 miles, depending on their intended use, but larger cruising motor and sailing boats can often have much greater range. Check that each boat you shortlist meets your needs. Do not forget to deduct the anticipated fuel consumption of generators, heaters etc for the period of the trip, and any fuel you cannot draw from the bottom of tanks, before dividing the quantity of fuel available by the consumption per hour and multiplying by cruising speed to arrive at the maximum range available to you.

If buying second hand and the engine(s) is out of manufacturer's warranty, insist on an engine trial. Consider getting a qualified marine engineer to carry out an inspection and trial on your behalf. If the engine(s) prove difficult to start or continue to smoke after warming up, and/or if the oil is very dirty, consider asking for a compression test. It is not very expensive and will give a good indication if there are problems with valves and/or piston rings. If the oil on the dipstick is emulsified (a milky brown colour) consult a marine engineer before proceeding further.

Used engines suffer more from lack of use than from regular use. A typical diesel engine, if well maintained, can be expected to have several thousand hours of running life, a petrol engine a little less. Four stroke outboards will probably have a longer life than two stroke, but it is usually corrosion of the alloys from which they are built which dictates an outboard's life. Any over 10 years old must be carefully inspected for bubbling paint, signs that indicate corrosion is occurring. Always carefully inspect past service records.

Rigs and Sails

These fall into four main categories; masts and spars, standing rigging, running rigging, and sails.

Masts and Spars

Masts are usually the longest-lasting items of this group; in fact it is quite unusual for a mast to be replaced. The most common reasons for replacement are a change to in-mast reefing, a change to a higher-tech racing mast, or replacement of a broken mast (possibly the result of rigging failure or impact). It is unusual for a mast to be replaced because of its age but not unusual for one to be serviced to avoid risk of failure. Masts are made of wood and carbon fibre but the most common material is aluminium alloy. Wooden masts are usually varnished and require regular time-consuming maintenance. Carbon fibre masts are usually only found on serious racing yachts, where their high cost is accepted in return for weight reduction high above the centre of gravity of the yacht. They are also occasionally found on the most expensive cruising sailing boats. Carbon fibre masts are usually self-coloured but some are painted to reduce ultra-violet effect. Aluminium masts should be built from marine-grade alloy; they are normally anodised finish clear, gold or white in colour, and on more expensive boats they are often painted. Personally, as painted masts are a constant corrosion battle, I recommend sticking to an anodised finish.

As the transverse rig base is too narrow for a wire between the chain plate (the attachment point for rigging at the deck) and the mast head to impart much by way of transverse stiffness to the rig, this is overcome by fitting spreaders (cross trees) at various positions up the mast. These allow a minimum transverse rigging to mast angle of around 10 degrees, which allows the shrouds (stays) to control transverse mast bending. Spreaders themselves very rarely break but their end fittings do need regular inspection.

Spars, booms, Genoa poles, spinnaker booms, jockey poles etc, usually manufactured from similar materials to the mast, again rarely give problems themselves but their end fittings need inspection and maintenance. Even for the cruising man, a carbon fibre spinnaker pole is worthy of consideration as its light weight makes for much easier handling.

Standing Rigging

Standing rigging has a service life and unfortunately, as the deterioration is often not readily visible, this is sometimes overlooked. As a guide, a cruising boat's standing rigging should be replaced at an interval of 10-15 years – less if the boat is very heavily used. A racing boat which will be stressed more regularly should have its standing rigging replaced at more regular intervals, normally between five and ten years, but if used for ocean passage racing, probably every 30,000 miles of sailing.

Standing rigging is manufactured from wire rope (usually 1 x 19 stainless steel construction), occasionally from Dyform® (which gives a higher proportion of steel in the same diameter and thus higher strength and less stretch), stainless steel or titanium rods (which give more strength and less stretch than wire but require greater care in use), or high-tech unidirectional fibre rope which can be difficult to terminate and has a short life expectancy, but is very strong and light with low stretch.

All standing rigging has to be tensioned. This is achieved using bottle screws (turnbuckles) for all standing rigging which does not require adjustment whilst sailing. Multi-purchase tackles, levers or hydraulic rams for standing rigging are used to alter fore and aft mast bend whilst sailing.

Running Rigging

Running rigging is the ropes used to hoist or trim the sails. This needs to be flexible for easy handling. Like standing rigging, running rigging has a limited life expectancy but unlike standing rigging, wear and defects are usually more readily seen. What you cannot see is loss of strength due to overstressing and ultra-violet action, so it is prudent to adopt a service by replacement programme based on a ten-year maximum life for lightly used cruisers, down to a two to three-season life for hard-used and highly stressed racing boats.

Running rigging used to be produced from a mix of flexible wire and fibre ropes but the development of high-tech fibres and the adoption of unidirectional rope construction with low stretch has all but eliminated wire (with added safety benefits). Consult a rigger as to which size and type of rope to use for each task, or buy a suitable publication.

When buying a new or used boat, check that all the rigging, spars and fittings necessary to operate with the sails you intend to set is available and in good, serviceable condition. On used boats, check the age and, if necessary, allow for replacement in your budget.

Mast, spar and rigging requirements will differ between the cruising and racing owner. The cruising owner will require a strong, simple rig with a minimum of at-sea adjustments necessary. Whilst not wanting excess weight aloft, it will be of less importance than to the racing owner. The cruising owner will require easily set sails which will probably mean built-in furling or reefing systems not requiring excessive effort or skill to use, due to limited crew. The racing owner will want a light rig, adjustable so that the centre of effort of the sail plan can be moved fore and aft and mainsail shape may be optimised to suit the conditions, and forestay tension can be increased upwind in stronger winds. Crew numbers and skill levels will allow use of these factors and more frequent sail plan changes.

Sails

The sails are the motor of a sailing boat. To the inexperienced they all look the same except the pretty coloured spinnakers, but the differences in shape and build are considerable. As mentioned above, the cruising boat owner is interested in strong, reliable, easily set sails. This does not mean they are any less important than the racing boat's sails, but it does mean they usually have to be capable of use over a wider wind range and more tolerant in adjustment. Most cruising boats will only require a limited number of sails: storm sails plus a mainsail, mizzen (if ketch, yawl or schooner), one headsail (or two if cutter rigged), probably furling on the forestays, and possibly one downwind sail, either a cruising chute or spinnaker. After all, a cruising owner has other uses for his storage space! A cruising boat's sails are usually of polyester construction as they are easier to handle and furl than high-tech cloths and probably have a longer life.

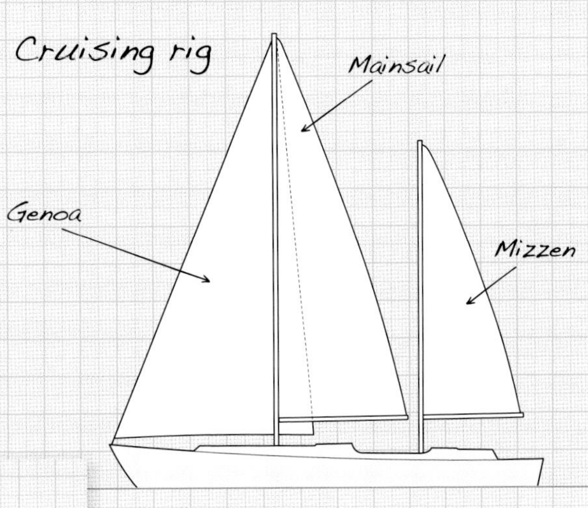
Cruising rig
Mainsail
Genoa
Mizzen

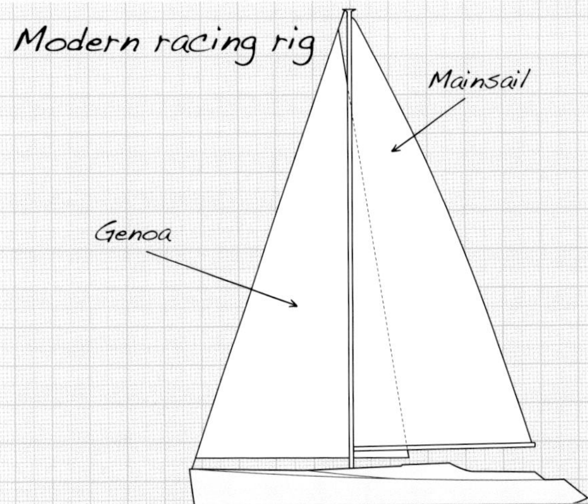
Modern racing rig
Mainsail
Genoa

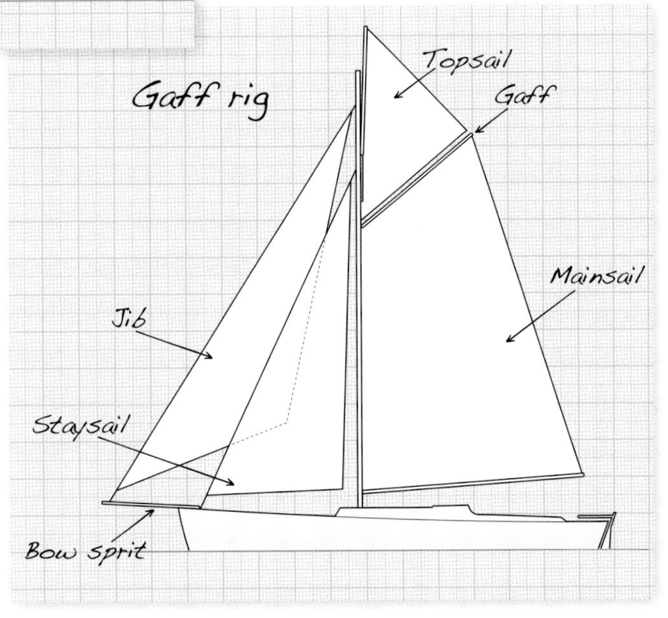
Gaff rig
Topsail
Gaff
Mainsail
Jib
Staysail
Bow sprit

New boats often come with one or two standard sails to which the owner adds as necessary to suit intended use. Furling gear and sails are sometimes options and sometimes standard. If sails are included in your new standard specification, take them, as the discount given if you do not is unlikely to reflect the true cost of buying a replacement set yourself. Used boats normally come with a wardrobe of sails. These can of course range from as-new through used but serviceable to only fit to be dust sheets! So check them carefully or, better still, have a sailmaker inspect them for you.

Racing boats will either be of one-design, restricted class or handicap rating type. One-design and/or restricted classes may well have class rules which dictate the number, type and size of sails you may use and some classes only allow the use of certain sailmakers in an effort to control cost. Check that sails supplied with a new or used boat meet class requirements. The number of different types of sails which can be carried on a handicap boat will be limited by the rating rule, i.e. a 40-foot boat may, in addition to her storm sails (which must be carried), be allowed for a race or series of races, a mainsail, five headsails and three downwind sails. New class boats are usually sold with sails included in the specification. New handicap rating boats normally have sails excluded from the specification. If you have to buy new racing sails, find out which product is doing well in sister ships, which sailmaker has good local service and is prepared to come aboard to test and check his product, and give you and your crew advice on how best to trim them.

You also have to set your spend level. This is one area where quality and reputation may cost more but will be a wise investment. Cloth choice should be discussed – high-tech cloths do hold better shape but need greater skill and care and unfortunately are not renowned for long life. Moulded sails are probably the ultimate but suffer similar cost, care and skill-level restrictions. However, if used properly, they will improve your chances of winning.

If buying a used racing boat she will probably come with many sails. Discount any over three years old as probably only suitable for delivery trips and any over one year old as good for training and the occasional club race. Any less than one year old can reasonably be expected to have a season's life in them, but if you are really serious about winning, add a new suit to your budget.

Deck Fittings

Most used boats, both motor and sail, will have their standard fit of deck fittings added to as necessary to equip the boat fully for her designed use, i.e. electric windlass, life raft stowage, deck cushions, awnings, upgraded winches. Most, on inspection, will show if they have proved up to their task. If over five years old it is worth considering if they are in need of service or replacement.

New boats' standard specifications, although adequate for basic use, do occasionally need upgrading to include items such as more powerful winches, covers, decking surfacing etc. This is particularly so on the more economy orientated models, which may also require some basic upgrades in the size of mooring cleats etc before they can be used with confidence. Once again, refer to your "objectives of ownership" to ensure your operating requirements are met.

Comfort Items

This section is mainly for the cruising owner. Cruising is meant to be relaxing enjoyment for you and your crew, so consider the items which will improve your boating and list them. You can then check if they are included in the specification of the new or used boats you shortlist and, if they are not, you can cost them into your budget of early post-purchase spending. Do not forget the system upgrades necessary to operate some comfort items. Your list may include:

Deck cushions
Bimini hoods
Teak decks
Hatch blinds and fly screens
Heating systems
Air conditioning
Ice maker
Washing machine
Wind generator
Microwave/steam oven
Boarding/stern ladder
Sound system
Special sprung mattresses
Powered winches

Cockpit or hatch cover
Cockpit tents
Deck seating and lockers
Circulation fans
Upgraded upholstery
Better/larger refrigeration/freezer
Water maker
Generator
Solar panels
Mood lighting
Television
Boat's tender
Deck shower
Electric furlers

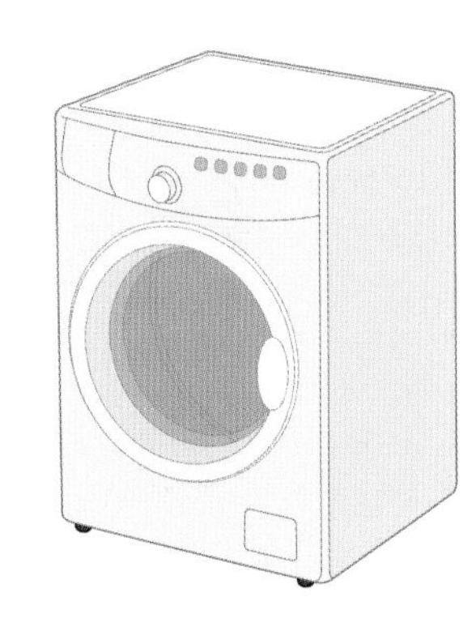

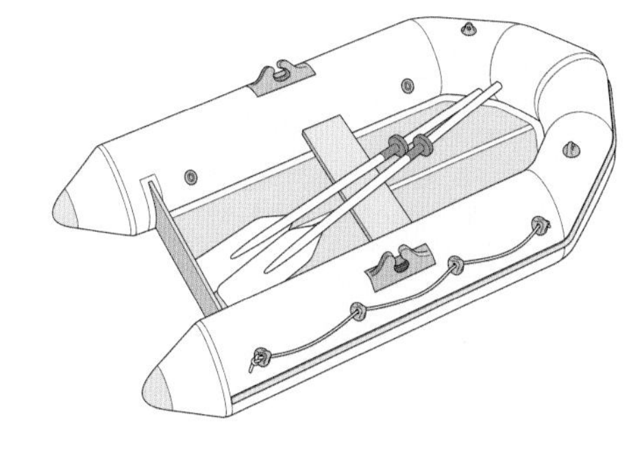

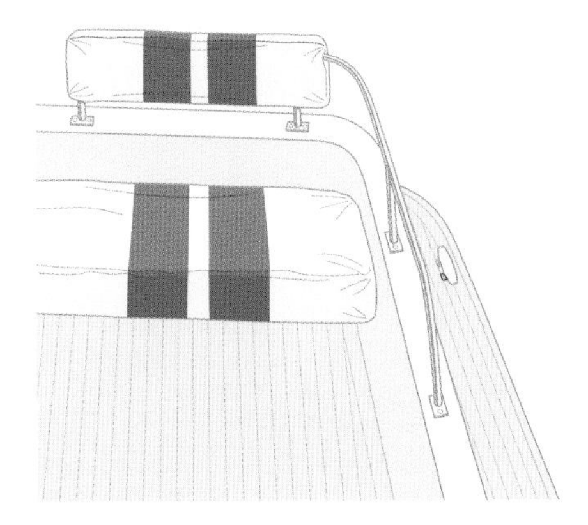

This may well call for an increase in battery capacity and, in turn, charging capacity. To check if battery capacity is adequate, add all the loads (in amps) of all DC consumers likely to be drawing from the domestic bank between rechargeable times, including lighting loads. Multiply this by the number of hours between charge times, (each item will be expected to be used). Now check the recommended maximum discharge percentage of your battery type and multiply by existing battery capacity to give your permitted available capacity between charges. If the between charge figure is greater than the permitted discharge figure, consider either larger batteries or cutting out loads. With new battery types recently becoming available which are more accepting of higher rates of charge and recover from deep discharge more readily than the old traditional lead acid batteries, it will be worth consulting a DC electrician relating to charging requirements. If buying used, remember traditional marine batteries have a life expectancy of between three and seven years, depending on quality and care in use.

A generator, if already fitted, may not have the capacity to run your additional equipment. A generator and diesel boat heater require extra fuel to run. All equipment takes up space, none more so than air conditioning with control panels, compressors, condensers and large-diameter ducting.

Electronic Navigational Aids

These must never be taken as an excuse to not fit or carry the basics of navigation, as electronics can always go wrong. You must always have a good magnetic compass with current deviation card, pencils, dividers, parallel rule, rubber, tide tables, almanac, charts etc.

That said, electronic aids have, in the last few years become considerably more reliable. Prices have dropped considerably and what used to be thought an expensive luxury is now not only affordable, but also far more capable and easier to use. The list is extensive and, as usual, I provide a guide below, but it may be out of date by the time you read this! Each owner will have to select the list which suits his/her objectives. For instance, a fisherman will almost certainly require a fish finder whereas a racing sailboat owner will not. Neither is radar likely to be high on a racing sailboat owner's shopping list, but it will certainly feature on a motor boat owner's list. Any sailing keel boat owner will deem essential a wind direction and speed indicator.

Log
Echo sounder
Wind direction and speed indicator
Fish finder
GPS
Chart plotter
Radar warning device
Gyro compass
Fluxgate compass
Radar
DSC VHF
Hand-held VHF
SSB radio
Sat C
Mini-M
Iridium
Navtex
Nav-Fax

Today, wind-depth transducers, a PC interfaced to a boat's GPS, and software with chart, tide, weather and boat's predicted-performance information giving real-time updates whilst racing and telling you when to tack, what wind speed, direction and tide to expect on the next leg, what sail to set, what course to steer and what speed to expect are available. I sail on a small boat with all this information available not only at the chart table, but also on a small waterproof touch-sensitive laptop on deck.

If you are buying a used boat, depending on age, you may wish to consider budgeting to replace old electronic equipment as it is often difficult to locate spares and service for out-of-production systems. Current equipment is usually more capable and reliable. New wireless logs, echo sounders and wind gear cut installation costs.

Trailers

This is not strictly boat equipment but if you intend to move your boat by road yourself, not only will you require a suitable road-legal trailer with light board, spare wheel and a spanner which fits the wheel nuts (this one caught me out once, as my truck wheel nuts were a different size from the trailer), but also a suitable towing vehicle. All cars, vans and trucks show the maximum towing weight either on a plate mounted on the vehicle or in the owner's handbook. This is the combined weight of boat, trailer and any kit carried in the boat. Beware though – some trailers were imported as complete outfits with boat and engine from the USA in the 1990s, which are not road legal in Europe. So check if offered one!

Top Tip

- If buying a trailer boat, check the boat's weight and whether the trailer weight is within your car's towing limit.

CHAPTER 8

Finding and Inspecting

One major factor which may well have a bearing on the methods used to find and inspect boats will be the timescale available to you. Obviously, unless you have already decided on a particular boat, you should allow a reasonable amount of time for this process. This will be to some extent dictated by the time of year that you start your search. In the UK the main boat shows take place in the autumn and winter, and the boating season between, say, April and September, when boats are being used, is not the ideal time to buy or sell. You may, however, have a fixed date by which you require your boat, for example for a race or a holiday, and this may well limit your pre-purchase time scale.

Top Tip

- Allow plenty of time to search within your purchase programme.

When putting your programme together, do not forget to allow the following three factors in your time calculations:

- New boats are often a little late on delivery.
- Used-boat contract completion tends to take weeks not days.
- For both new and used boats, you will need two or three weeks' familiarisation and trials before undertaking a serious race or cruise.

By now you should have various lists and notes, your objectives of ownership, types or classes of boats which suit your needs, your budget allowance, size limitations, whether you are buying new, used or either and prioritised equipment lists. These will allow you to quickly eliminate unsuitable boats in your quest.

If you are buying new, the places to look include magazines. Some are inclined to cater for particular sections of the sport so concentrate on those suited to your preferred mode of boating. Boat shows, the internet, boat showrooms and clubs should provide the information necessary for you to get into contact with builders and/or their distributors, agents or dealers. If you have already selected a class of boat, enquire if it has an owners club or class association and, if it does, contact this body as they will not only be able to provide further information on the boat, but may also have listings of boats available and associated equipment for sale.

If you are buying used, in addition to the contact points mentioned above, you will want to contact brokerage offices (often found in marinas and boatyards). Again, be selective, as certain brokers specialise in particular classes, makes and types of boat. It could well pay to find out if any second-hand boat shows are scheduled within your search period, as these concentrate boats that are seriously for sale in one location.

Brokers do not usually own the boats that they offer for sale and simply act for the owner as his agent trying to sell his property. They should be able to provide you with a set of details for the boats they have on offer and solicit from the owner any further information you may require. As with a number of specialists, there are a few less-reputable operatives around, so with boat sales companies, brokers and surveyors, it is worth checking that they belong to a reputable trade association. Although no absolute guarantee of their integrity, trade bodies do try to weed out unprincipled traders. You can check if a trader is a member of an appropriate trade body by contacting either the Royal Yachting Association on 023 8060 4100 or The British Marine Federation on 01784 473377. From the information you can obtain from these sources you should be in a position to form a list of new or used boats which you believe may meet your objectives, budget etc.

Top Tip

- Consult genuine experts on your type of boat and listen to friends, but remember that their views may be biased towards their own objectives.

At this point you should also use your own judgement to eliminate any boats which, whilst meeting your broad criteria on paper, you simply do not like! As the result of looks, reputation or design, first impressions are important and it is unlikely that you will ever be happy with a boat on which you had initial reservations.

At this stage you may wish to consult friends, crew or experts of your acquaintance for their advice and guidance. However, be careful how much faith you put in their suggestions as it is natural for anyone to put their own ideas and objectives forward when giving advice and there is no reason these should necessarily coincide with your reasons for purchase. As a boat supplier, I was always wary when an owner said he had a friend who was an "expert" yachtsman who was helping him set his specification. Sometimes this friend was a genuine expert and gave good, sound guidance, but more often than not the friend was far from an expert and, even when he was, his own priorities tended to cloud his judgement as to what was required to meet the owner's needs and budget.

Top Tip

- Keep a written and photographic record of each boat`s condition and equipment, or you will soon mix up boats you have inspected.

As time permits, plan to visit as many boats on your list as possible. Make notes on each one, as after only two or three you will get confused as to what you liked or disliked about each. Plan your inspection trips to incorporate all the prospective boats on one river, yard or marina at one time. Tend to make these initial inspections short, simply ruling boats in or out from your list. Remember that the next boat may be perfect for you, so do not risk running out of time and not getting to see her while you spend too much time inspecting and discussing a boat that in your heart you know is not right for you. There are many boats out there and given the time and willingness you will be bound to find your dream one!

If possible keep a photograph of each boat you believe has a chance of making your shortlist, for future reference.

When inspecting boats, always remember that they are someone's personal property, so ask permission from the owner or broker before stepping aboard. Also, they are probably stored on private property, so ask before entering. The property owner has a duty of care to the boat owner so do not be surprised if you get shouted at for going aboard without asking. The property owner will also be responsible for safe access so again he/she will not be happy if you build your own makeshift ladder out of old blocks and oil drums to get aboard.

From this process you will probably end up with a reasonably long list of boats that you have not as yet ruled out.

CHAPTER 9

Shortlisting

The object of this exercise is to reduce your list of boats which may suit you to a list of only three to five boats which definitely meet most of your requirements and which you are prepared to spend further consideration and inspection time on.

Top Tip

- Keep your short list short – 5 boats as an absolute maximum.

Check each of the long list boats against your notes, setting out your desires and budgets. Check which have specifications nearest to your wishes and cost in any high-priority items not included in the specification on offer to get a true comparative cost.

Eliminate any boat seriously above your budget. Any boat making it onto your shortlist should be one you would not object to owning.

CHAPTER 10

What is a fair price?

Before you proceed further towards final inspection and making an offer on any of your shortlisted boats, you should decide what you believe is a fair price for each. Doing so at this stage will avoid you being lured into offering too high a price. Ensure that you have considered all cost implications of purchase and have the tools to hand to substantiate the level of any offer you make, possibly by highlighting the financial benefits of other shortlisted boats to the sales man. To do this, refer to your objectives of ownership and your budget calculations.

Take into account, when arriving at your fair price, the prices quoted for near sister ships, or boats of the same class, and the specification included in the price. If new boats feature on your list, one-design boats are less inclined to be discounted than economic production boats, which often attract special deals at boat shows. Quality boats do not normally have the same selling discount percentage built into their prices as do the less expensive production boats. Discount structures vary from builder to builder and with model popularity, so it is difficult to give hard guidelines as to what to expect to achieve off a list price. A new boat from a top-quality builder may be bought, after haggling, at between 2.5-7.5% off the list price, and an economy production boat at between 5-15% off, depending on its current popularity. Dealers could offer additional equipment and, provided you had the equipment offered on your intended specification, this may prove beneficial.

Top Tip

- For each shortlisted boat take time to arrive at a fair price based on age, condition, fitted equipment etc by comparison to other available boats.

Except on the smallest of boats, be very wary if you are offered any discount over 15%, as this is certainly not normal and may indicate an unpopular model, a boat with an unpopular colour or specification, or a dealer with problems.

Second-hand boats are more difficult to arrive at a fair price for, particularly if there are not many sister ships on the market to compare prices with. In this situation one has to resort to considering the prices of boats of similar type, age and quality.

Condition and quantity of included equipment also have a bearing on fair price. There are really only two things you can do – either consult a professional valuation expert, but his figure may be given with so many ifs, buts, ands and ors that you may think your fee has gained you little; or spend time doing comparisons from magazines and brokerage listings yourself.

CHAPTER 11

Final inspections and making an offer

Contact the person or company responsible for each of the boats on your shortlist. Let them know that you have a serious interest in the boat in question and that you wish to carry out a full inspection yourself prior to making an offer to purchase. Ask that they have all relevant documents ready for your inspection. These may include a list of items included in the sale price, specification, class or rating certificate (if applicable), registration documentation (if applicable), service history, any licences or test certificates, and a Recreational Craft Directive certificate if new or of recent build. Ask for confirmation of what drawings, owner's manuals etc are available with the boat. This is as much to ascertain her level of previous care if used, or the seller's professionalism if new, as for the information itself. Let the seller know that you have a shortlist and that this is one of several boats you will be viewing. This may induce him to sharpen his focus and to take time on your enquiry.

Top Tip

- When making your offer, stipulate what conditions you attach to the offer, such as trials, survey, delivery time and repairs to be completed by current owner.

If it is a new boat you have shortlisted, ask for a sea trial. It is unusual to seek a trial with a used boat before an offer has been made and provisionally accepted, and then if the trial involves some costs, such as launching, you may well be asked to contribute if the sale does not proceed. Fix mutually agreeable dates and make it clear an agreed trial date is subject to prevailing weather being reasonable. Should you need to alter the date, give the maximum warning possible.

When you arrive for each inspection or trial, be appropriately dressed with deck shoes available and take all your notes related to this boat, a pad and pen to make more notes, and a camera. It may be a good idea to take a set of overalls or old clothes for bilge and engine space inspection. You will need to concentrate on the task in hand, so if you take young children make sure there is someone to keep them safe and from distracting you. Do not turn up with your whole crew and their partners, as you will accomplish little.

Ask all relevant questions, including history, if the boat is second hand and about warranty details if new. If the sales person is unable to answer important questions at the time of inspection, request that he finds the answers and passes them to you. Invent a time scale if you do not have one. Make sure he knows this boat is not your only option but if, after viewing, you decide to rule this boat out of your shortlist let him know. Do not give too detailed a reason or he will try to talk you around. If you have decided not to proceed with this boat you will require a very strong reason to have a change of mind.

If you are still interested, let him know but I recommend you do not proceed to making any step towards an offer until you have inspected all boats on your shortlist.

If your shortlist includes privately advertised second-hand boats, other than boats under 25 feet (8m) where due to their relative value private sales are quite normal, question the reason for a private sale. It may be an owner reasonably trying to save cost, or there may be a more sinister reason related to title or build approvals etc. If you think this boat is the one for you, to avoid risk, appoint either a lawyer or broker to carry out all relevant checks and ensure there are no hidden problems.

Having decided which of the boats from your list best suits your objectives, the time has come to make an offer. Make one final check that your finances can stand the expenditure you are about to commit to, including checking with your finance company (if appropriate) that the level of loan you will require for this boat and associated costs is within their lending limits for both you and this type of boat.

Consult your objectives, equipment requirements and budget one more time. Does this boat meet your main objectives of ownership, or have you been sweet-talked into considering a boat inappropriate for you? Will she have all the major items of equipment you require and, if not, have you included them in your total spend as opposed to just purchase price budget? Does it look like you stand a good chance of getting her total purchase price within your budget? Finally and most importantly, are you happy at the prospect of becoming the owner of this boat? If not, stop now and start to look elsewhere.

Formulate your offer.

If on a used boat, add up all the items of equipment that you need and are not included in her specification. You can use them and the lower prices of any similar sister or near sisters to substantiate any reduction in asking price you put forward, but be careful. If the current asking price is reasonable someone else may offer the full or nearer to full price and steal the boat from under your nose, forcing you to find another boat.

Make your offer subject to survey and sea trials. You may wish to have major items such as sails and/or engine(s) surveyed in addition to the normal hull survey. Pick your surveyor with care; choose someone who has experience on the type of boat you are buying. Seek the broker's advice if necessary on this. If, after sea trials and survey, there are major items of concern, you can either make your offer firm but subject to their correction, or reduce your offer price to reflect the cost of making good emergent defects.

Top Tip

- If you are making an offer below the asking price it is a good idea to explain the reason for the reduction, but keep it short, as you may want a second reduction after trials or survey.

Always check that your surveyor has professional liability insurance. A good broker working to his professional bodies' standards will ensure that there is clear title to the boat, that she is free from debt such as an undischarged mortgage, that all her ship's papers are in order, that the funds only change hands at the appropriate time, and that she has all her appropriate VAT documentation and was not previously owned by a company which reclaimed the VAT, making her possibly liable for a further payment.

Unless you intend to own a fleet, only make an offer on one boat at a time. Do not waste people's time with silly offers or offers which are beyond your means. Unless you must have this particular boat and are not prepared to be outbid, do try a lower offer. Usually a discount of 10% or less will not be seen as an insult.

If offering on a new boat, give the salesman your wish list of equipment not included within the specification on offer. Also indicate what level of discount you expect and ask him to think how he can best satisfy your requirements. Do not give him more than a day or two to consider. Let him come back to you with an offer. If it is below or very near to your budget, try to get one or two final concessions, possibly a period of free berthing or some safety kit you are short of, before closing the deal. Do not forget to obtain confirmation of delivery date and to agree fair payment terms which protect your investment.

Top Tip

- Decide whether you are prepared to love, honour and dedicate a large part of your hard-earned cash and time to this boat. If yes, proceed with the purchase. If no, walk away from this one.

One area I have not previously mentioned is part exchange. This has never been common in brokerage deals and is even less likely now than in the past, due to new consumer legislation making a dealer who owns a boat obliged to offer some kind of warranty in most cases. On new boats, part exchange is sometimes possible but usually only if you are purchasing a more expensive boat than the one you are selling, and if the boat you are selling is from a model range represented by the dealer. You will almost certainly get a better price for your used boat if you sell her through brokerage. Some dealers will offer a fallback buy-in price for your boat if she is not sold on brokerage by the time an instalment on the new boat falls due, but this is likely to reflect a heavily discounted value.

Keep written confirmed records of all matters relating to the final transaction.

CHAPTER 12

Reminders for early days of ownership

Congratulations! You are now the proud owner of a boat, selected to suit your personal requirements.

Is she insured by you? Strangely, there is no legal requirement to insure a private boat, but most boatyards and marinas will only let boats with adequate third-party cover onto their premises and all marine mortgage companies will insist on sighting your insurance papers, probably requiring their interest in the boat to be noted. Make sure your cover is relevant to your use, i.e. area of use, type of use, racing risks if necessary. Assuming you are insuring fully comprehensive (almost all do), make sure you include all equipment costs. You may also wish to consider taking out a policy to cover your crew against personal injury whilst aboard.

Sort out your berthing arrangements if you have not already done so. Take time to familiarise yourself and your crew with your new boat, her equipment, safety gear and systems before embarking on long passages or serious racing. Buy tools, spares and domestic equipment not included in the purchase.

Select your crew and give them maximum advance warning of your next year's boating plans. When selecting crew, ensure all major skills required are covered and, if possible, duplicated. Get your crew to commit their time, and ensure they are compatible.

Check past servicing if you bought second hand, and set up a service programme for the next year. Check that all licences – radio etc, and all safety equipment is in date. Set up contacts with your various service providers so that you know who to contact for service and repairs, as and when the need arises.

Good boating!

IT'S ALL ABOUT YOU AND THE BOATING YOU DO

RYA MEMBERSHIP APPLICATION

Be part of it

One of boating's biggest attractions is its freedom from rules and regulations. As an RYA member you'll play an active part in keeping it that way, as well as benefiting from free expert advice and information, plus discounts on a wide range of boating products, charts and publications.

To join the RYA, please complete the application form below and send it to The Membership Department, RYA, RYA House, Ensign Way, Hamble, Southampton, Hampshire SO31 4YA. You can also join online at www.rya.org.uk, or by phoning the membership department on +44 (0) 23 8060 4159. Whichever way you choose to apply, you can save money by paying by Direct Debit. A Direct Debit instruction is on the back of this form.

	Title	Forename	Surname	Gender	Date of Birth
Applicant 1					/ /
Applicant 2					/ /
Applicant 3					/ /
Applicant 4					/ /

E-mail Applicant 1

E-mail Applicant 2

E-mail Applicant 3

E-mail Applicant 4

Address

Post Code

Home Tel

Day Time Tel

Mobile Tel

Type of membership required (Tick Box)

- **Junior (0-11)** Annual rate £5 or **£5 if paying by Direct Debit**
- **Youth (12-17)** Annual rate £14 or **£11 if paying by Direct Debit**
- **Under 25** Annual rate £25 or **£22 if paying by Direct Debit**
- **Personal** Annual rate £43 or **£39 if paying by Direct Debit**
- **Family*** Annual rate £63 or **£59 if paying by Direct Debit**

Save money by completing the Direct Debit form overleaf

Please number up to three boating interests in order, with number one being your principal interest

- Yacht Racing
- Yacht Cruising
- Dinghy Racing
- Dinghy Cruising
- Personal Watercraft
- Sportboats & RIBs
- Windsurfing
- Motor Boating
- Powerboat Racing
- Canal Cruising
- River Cruising

* *Family Membership: 2 adults plus any under 18s all living at the same address. Prices valid until 30/9/2011*
One discount voucher is accepted for individual memberships, and two discount vouchers are accepted for family membership.

IMPORTANT In order to provide you with membership benefits the details provided by you on this form and in the course of your membership will be maintained on a database. If you do not wish to receive information on member services and benefits please tick here ☐. By applying for membership of the RYA you agree to be bound by the RYA's standard terms and conditions (copies on request or at www.rya.org.uk)

Signature

Date / /

Source Code

Joining Point Code

GET MORE FROM **YOUR BOATING** SUPPORT THE **RYA**

PAY BY DIRECT DEBIT – AND SAVE MONEY

Instructions to your Bank or Building Society to pay by Direct Debit

Please fill in the form and send to:

Membership Department, Royal Yachting Association, RYA House, Ensign Way, Hamble, Southampton, Hampshire SO31 4YA.

Name and full postal address of your Bank/Building Society

To the Manager	Bank/Building Society
Address	
	Postcode

Name(s) of Account Holder(s)

Branch Sort Code ☐☐ – ☐☐ – ☐☐

Bank/Building Society Account Number ☐☐☐☐☐☐☐☐

Originator's Identification Number

9	5	5	2	1	3

DIRECT Debit

RYA Membership Number (For office use only)

Instructions to your Bank or Building Society

Please pay Royal Yachting Association Direct Debits from the account detailed in this instruction subject to the safeguards assured by The Direct Debit Guarantee. I understand that this instruction may remain with the Royal Yachting Association and, if so, details will be passed electronically to my Bank/Building Society.

Signature(s)

Date: / /